Tide of the Supernatural

A Call to Love the Muslim World

KUNDAN L. MASSEY
Director
Lifeagape International in the Middle East

Scripture quotations are from the New American Standard Bible unless stated otherwise. Copyright © The Lockman Foundation, 1960, 1962, 1963, 1968, 1971, 1972, 1973. Used by permission.

Other versions used include the New English Bible (NEB), the Living Bible (LB), and the Good News Bible (GNB).

TIDE OF THE SUPERNATURAL
by Kundan L. Massey

Published by Here's Life Publishers, Inc.,
the publishing ministry of
Campus Crusade for Christ International,
P.O. Box 1576, San Bernardino, CA 92402

ISBN 0-918956-70-6
HLP Product No. 95-021-2

With my prayer that their lives may continue to be characterized by the supernatural to the glory of Jesus Christ, I dedicate this book

To IQBAL KUNDAN MASSEY, my beloved wife and life's partner, through whose love, sacrifice and faithful prayers my life and ministry have been increasingly blessed, and without whose encouragement this book could not have been written.

and

To SHALEM ASHER MASSEY, my only son, who has grown up in this ministry in the Middle East, bearing with us the difficulties of long separations for Jesus' sake.

ACKNOWLEDGMENTS

The preparation of this book truly has been characterized by the supernatural. It was three short months after I was convinced that such a book needed to be written that our manuscript was finalized and into the hands of the publishers. Considering the pace at which things usually happen here in the Middle East, it is certainly through God's grace and the faithful prayer support of so many of our co-laborers that we were able to finish the book in such a short time.

I praise God for the cooperative spirit and efforts of my entire Middle East staff in the production of this book, especially those in the Middle East headquarters. In particular, I wish to express my deep thanks to Barbara Baker, Lurabelle Annis and my beloved wife, Iqbal Massey, for their many hours of hard work in the essential research and drafting of the manuscript. I have also appreciated the fine cooperation and professional assistance of David L. Orris and his staff at Here's Life Publishers in speeding along the publication of this book.

Throughout the writing of this book, the loving encouragement of Bill and Vonette Bright has provided constant confirmation to me that God wants me to share the miracles that He has begun through the Middle East Leadership Fellowship. It is my sincere prayer that this book will glorify only my Master, Jesus Christ, and help to accelerate the fulfillment of His Great Commission in the Middle East.

FOREWORD

In the course of the last few years, the Middle East has become one of the most powerful, if unpredictable, regions of the world. And yet today the tide of the supernatural is sweeping across the Middle East as never before.

I state this with confidence because of my recent participation in a strategic gathering of Middle Eastern Christians which I believe is beginning already to revolutionize the course of history in the Middle East, perhaps more than any other single event in this century. I refer to the Middle East Leadership Fellowship — the personal vision of Kundan Massey, and the unique occasion for this book. If you question the optimism of my statement, I would invite you to read this account carefully, particularly the responses in Chapter 15 from individuals who participated in this unprecedented gathering.

There are few Middle Eastern Christians who are making a more significant contribution to the fulfillment of the Great Commission in the Muslim world than Kundan Massey. Throughout his more than 20 years of active ministry in the Middle East and Asia, since he first launched the Pakistan Campus Crusade for Christ ministry in 1959, Kundan has acquired a deep and unique compassion for the Muslim peoples of the world. As the director of Middle East affairs for our ministry, he faces some of the most staggering impossibilities of our generation with regard to helping fulfill the Great Commission in the Middle East.

It is my prayer that as you read this remarkable account of the moving of God's Holy Spirit across the Middle East — and in particular the miracles of the highly significant Middle East Leadership Fellowship — you will join Kundan Massey in a bold new love for the Middle East, a region now experiencing a great tide of the supernatural.

Dr. Bill Bright
President and Founder
Campus Crusade for Christ International

INTRODUCTION

Although I have ministered for the sake of Jesus Christ in the Middle East since 1959, I have become increasingly aware over the past five years that God is moving in a very wonderful, supernatural way at this particular time in this strategic area of the world.

Despite the political upheaval, the increasing instability and the tension which characterize the situation in the Middle East in the daily news, the Spirit of God is bringing together an opportunity for what I believe will be the greatest spiritual harvest in the Middle East since the Lord Jesus Christ came here to live, die and rise again.

I am not alone in this confidence, for it was my privilege, in November of 1979, to watch a new spirit of faith and optimism sweep across a representative group of national believers from throughout the Middle East. They were gathered in Nicosia, Cyprus, for the Middle East Leadership Fellowship, an incredible vision and dream which God gave to me and which prompted the writing of this book.

It is my prayer that this book will motivate you, with new compassion and understanding, to believe God with us for a supernatural saturation of the Middle East with the loving Good News of our Lord Jesus Christ.

Kundan Massey

TABLE OF CONTENTS

Kundan Massey inscribes the name of Jesus on the sands of Saudi Arabia

CHAPTER
ONE

A Supernatural Imprint

"For the vision is yet for the appointed time; it hastens
toward the goal, and it will not fail. Though it tarries,
wait for it; for it will certainly come, it will not delay."

Habakkuk 2:3

"We have lost our son, our only son!"

I stared at my distraught wife, hardly comprehending her words as she sobbed them out.

The night before Tehran had gone wild. With the new Iranian revolution just declared in early February of 1979, the populace had gone to battle with what remained of the fallen Shah's forces. It had seemed that the city itself were on fire, as dark clouds of smoke formed an ominous haze across the cold winter landscape.

Nearly everyone on the street brandished a gun, even small boys, and as I had returned that morning from a fruitless attempt to obtain air tickets for evacuation, I saw confiscated army jeeps from the imperial garrisons careening through the city. Shouting and shooting their guns in the air, the civilian riders stopped at various intersections to encourage and even coerce young volunteers to join them in ransacking government offices and palaces.

So I already was unnerved, as I returned to the friend's home where we had taken refuge a few days before, to discover my wife in tears over the disappearance of our teenage son, Shalem.

"I shouldn't have sent him to the store," she sobbed, "but we needed at least some milk and yogurt for today!"

When he did not return after a few minutes, she had consoled herself that surely he had just gone on to the next shop down the street. But when more than an hour passed, the panic rose steadily in her heart. Where could he be?

My first response was a mental picture of those roaming jeeps, picking up every young man in sight, and fear struck my own heart. Shalem was only 16, but he was as tall as I was, and

1

he could have been mistaken so easily for an Iranian.

We fell on our knees together with God's Word open before us, pleading for supernatural comfort and a promise to cling to for our missing son. Iqbal's eyes fell on the familiar words of John 3:16: "For God so loved the world, that He gave His only begotten Son, that whoever believes in Him should not perish, but have eternal life."

The words were like a dagger to her heart and mine. We wept unashamed, understanding in a completely new dimension the Calvary love of God the Father when He gave His only Son. What a price to pay! In agony, we wondered if we were about to be asked to give up our only son, right here in the Middle East where we had lived and ministered for the sake of Christ for so many years.

God graciously comforted our burdened hearts by showing us His promise in Isaiah 41:10: "Do not fear, for I am with you; do not look anxiously about you, for I am your God. I will strengthen you, surely I will help you, surely I will uphold you with My righteous right hand."

Obediently, through our tears, we prayed the hardest prayer we have ever had to pray: "Thank You, Father. Thank You that Shalem is gone, and we don't know where he is. Thank You that he is in Your righteous right hand, and so are we. Thank You."

The minutes that followed were agonizing ones, but we were cushioned in a supernatural way by the peace of God Himself. Another half hour went by before finally, around the corner at another intersection, I spotted the tall form of my son, leaning casually against a light pole as he conversed in Farsi with a jeepload of armed students! Overcome with joy, I rushed over to him and quickly steered him back to the house, into the arms of his mother.

Personal Dimension

Through this experience, God gave me a very personal dimension to my understanding of Christ's Great Commission. For years, I had signed my letters, "Together with you in His command to GO. . ." But in a powerful way, through the possible loss of my own son, God reminded me that Jesus had concluded His unconditional command to "go" with the strongest possible promise: "Lo, I am with you always." It is

The Massey family —
Kundan and Iqbal
with their son,
Shalem.

no matter that we risk our property, our lives and the lives of those dear to us — because Jesus goes with us, through every heartache and difficulty.

This sobering incident only underscored my commitment to the fulfillment of the Great Commission in the Middle East, the "impossible" task toward which I had invested my life for many years. My burden and vision had continued to deepen in even more specific terms after 1975, when Dr. Bill Bright, the president and founder of Campus Crusade for Christ, gave me the responsibility of directing this ministry in the Middle East.

I remember so well my response to his challenge, after a night alone with God in prayer. "We have only a very few Christians in the Middle East," I told Dr. Bright. "But when we train them, you will see how these little lights will become a big light for Jesus Christ!"

During the past few years, I have searched out these "little lights," small handfuls of believers in almost every nation and sheikdom of the Middle East. As I met them in small groups or fellowships, I began sharing with them some of the same concepts and training which have transformed my own spiritual life over the years. Wherever I went — along the Gulf, up into pockets of North Africa, or through populous nations like Pakistan and Egypt — I heard them voicing a common plea for training. These dear brothers and sisters in Christ were eager to hear everything I could share with them. "We haven't heard these wonderful things before!" they would exclaim, after I had shared a simple message on how to "breathe spiritually," or demonstrated how to share their faith in Christ in simple, clear terms.

I found that a number of those who called themselves Christians by their birth and heritage had yet to experience the reality of the new birth, even as I had been a "nominal Christian" until my college years. Even more were confused about how to appropriate the power of the Holy Spirit in their daily lives, and most were so intimidated by their surrounding circumstances that they were afraid to witness for Jesus Christ among their neighbors and friends. In fact, most of them were just like me 25 years ago — they had come to know and love Jesus Christ in a very precious way, but they really did not know how to share God's love in a clear way so that another person could receive Christ.

Yet we knew that we were the ones Jesus had told to hold up the Light of the world and to be the salt of the earth among our own people. Yes, the Middle Eastern believers were few in number, and isolated, and in some cases persecuted — but we clearly were called by God to help reach our own nations with His love.

The Vision is Born

In the West, the Christian world was beginning to awaken to the great neglect of the Middle East so far as missionary efforts and indigenous ministry were concerned. Even so, most of the emphasis and talk seemed to be about evangelism. How are we going to communicate the gospel in the Middle East — over the radio, or through printed tracts, or by direct mail letters, or with evangelistic films, or by distributing New Testaments, or what? But at that point, it seemed that very few were considering how to train the national believers in depth, so that they would become strong, effective witnesses for Christ *as a way of life!*

I realized that once our national believers actually took the leadership in evangelizing and discipling their own people, they would silence the common objection of Middle Eastern peoples, "Oh, Christianity is a western religion!" Too many Muslims today somehow have the idea that Jesus was born in London or New York, rather than in Bethlehem! With all my heart, I wanted to see the Lord Jesus Christ become a Middle Easterner once again in the thinking and understanding of all the peoples of the Middle East. However, I knew that this could only happen as the Middle Eastern believers were trained and committed to allow the love of Christ to flow through their own lives.

So my thoughts and prayers began to focus with more and more intensity upon a unique vision God had planted in my heart during my travels over a concentrated period of several months — a vision for a gathering of national Christian leaders from the entire Middle East. Such a representative gathering of believers — Arabs of every nationality, Pakistanis, Persians and even large tribal groups — had never been attempted in the past century, and maybe never. But surely a conference of this nature would be a vital catalyst to the spread of the gospel of Christ's love across the Middle East.

By convening the national believers ministering in the Muslim world, it would knit together our hearts and minds in the love, unity and cooperative spirit that must characterize all involved in the fulfillment of our Lord's Great Commission in this difficult area of the world. Most of all, it would provide the very training in the Spirit-filled Christian life, prayer, witnessing, discipleship and management that national believers had been requesting again and again in recent years. I could see that if even a few hundred key national Christians representing all the nations of the Middle East were to attend and catch this vision for strong national ministries that are characterized by the supernatural, they could return home to multiply the vision many times over among the believers in their own countries.

At the same time, I began to pray that God would use such a significant gathering to dissolve in our hearts any last "faith barrier" that might loom before us in regard to reaching the Middle Eastern peoples with the love of Jesus Christ in our generation. For me, that last "faith barrier" had been Saudi Arabia, the heartland of Islam . . .

The Impossible Visa

I had wondered whether we'd even be able to make that trip to Saudi Arabia in the spring of 1978. Saudi Arabia is one of a number of Middle Eastern nations where there are no known national believers, and where Christian missionaries are denied entrance. Even though I have valid teaching credentials and degrees to back up my occupational I.D. on visa forms as "teacher — management training," invitations from within the country were required and hard to come by.

My wife and I had been invited by several congregations of expatriate believers (Arabic-, English- and Urdu-speaking individuals) to minister among them for a few days. We had set dates many weeks ahead for the prayer seminars my wife would lead and the various groups of believers with whom I would share the ministry of the Holy Spirit. We were also anxious to meet again with the small congregation of Urdu believers which we had helped to form on our visit the previous year. They had started with just a few attenders, and we had heard it had now grown considerably.

But despite letters and cables informing us that the visa invitations were en route, the Saudi Arabian Embassy near our home in Tehran insisted they had not received them. In fact, when I presented my passport at the embassy, explaining that our visas had been cabled from Dhahran, the official asked shortly, "Are you a Muslim or a Christian?"

"I am a Christian," I responded.

"Then you cannot have this visa!" he declared, returning my passport across the desk. He would not even look to see if my visa had been cabled. Finally he shoved some forms at me and said, "If you want to, you can fill out these visa applications. I don't think you can get a visa, because we don't give any without an invitation, and you don't have one!" I stood there, sure that our visas were there somewhere, but also convinced that the man didn't want to find them. So I thanked him and went home.

I was very discouraged, but as I shared with my wife how this man had insulted me, she responded, "He did not insult you. He insulted Jesus Christ. So let's praise God for this man. God will change his heart and give us the visas!"

The next day was the prophet Muhammad's birthday, a national holiday in Iran and most of the Middle East. So the following day I returned to the Saudi embassy with praise in my heart, confident that God could and would change this man's heart.

Even so, I was amazed when I entered the embassy's visa

office to have this same man get up and walk clear across the room to greet me! He had recognized me immediately, and he said, "Mr. Massey, I am so sorry that I insulted you the other day, and I talked to you very badly."

"It's all right," I told him, thanking God with all my heart for his new attitude.

Drawing me over to his desk, the official continued, "I want you to know that I really did not do the right thing to you the other day, and I am very glad that you came back. Because you already have your air tickets, we can give you a transit visa for three days." So he stamped the visas in our passports, and I hurried home to pack my suitcase, rejoicing in the power of praising God!

Prison Experience

Soon after we arrived in Saudi Arabia, we learned that God had performed another unusual miracle — this time for the young Arab member of our Lifeagape staff who had flown in to minister with us during our visit. This young man had been jailed when he arrived at the airport, since his father who lived in Saudi Arabia had misunderstood his arrival time and failed to meet him with the necessary visa documents.

The immigration authorities were confused over the location of his visa, but they were also upset over some of his answers to their questions. When asked his religion, he responded by saying, "Well, I am a child of God, through Jesus Christ." That only made the situation worse. So they put him in prison overnight, refusing him water or any comforts until his visa was produced the next morning by his father.

This young man endured the whole experience with a trusting heart, telling me afterwards, "If they had only known who I really am — a child of the King — they would have been afraid to touch me!" Even so, it was a bit of a shock for this young man, who had returned only weeks before from finishing his university education in the United States.

"It's hard for me, as a modern Arab, to realize that this sort of thing still happens all the time here in the Middle East!" he admitted.

One Name on the Sand

I had visited the cities of Saudi Arabia a number of times

before, but on this particular trip we drove at length through the endless stretches of the Desert Kingdom. It was hard to believe that under these dry sands lay the largest proven crude oil reserves in the world — the "black gold" of petroleum which ranks Saudi Arabia as one of the world's major oil-producing nations.

"Let's write the name of Jesus here!" exclaimed the tall Arab believer standing at my side. So we stooped together and wrote a huge "JESUS" with our hands in the sand. Then we stood in silence, watching the hot, blowing sands cover our letters. Unsatisfied, we bent down again and once more inscribed "Jesus," this time in deeper, wider strokes.

We were all touched and quiet, until finally my wife suggested that we take a picture. I agreed, and after setting the camera I knelt on the sand by the name of my Savior and Lord. Suddenly a persistent question welled up in my heart: "Will the name of Jesus ever be inscribed on these sands of Saudi Arabia? How will these Arabs ever hear?"

Tears came to my eyes, and as I looked down, it was as though the letters were stained in red. I knew that God was reminding me that the blood of Jesus Christ was shed to saturate all the thirsty sands of Saudi Arabia, along with the rest of the Middle East and the world.

"Yes, Father," I prayed in my heart. "I believe that *even here* in the heartland of Islam, You will inscribe the name of Jesus Christ all over the sands."

By the time we returned to the jeep and started on our way again, I knew that the name "Jesus" was covered over by the blowing sands. Yet it still remained, imprinted on my mind and heart.

That imprint has never left my life, for that day I saw my last "faith barrier" in the Middle East come tumbling down. No longer did my burden for the Muslim world leave my heart restless and overwhelmed, for my thoughts and prayers were filled with a growing excitement for the vision God had given me to help gather together and train my fellow believers in the Middle East. I could hardly wait for the opportunity to share with Christians from all over the Middle East the same training that had revolutionized my own walk with Jesus Christ since I had first met Him in Pakistan . . .

CHAPTER
TWO

Opening the Door

". . . If anyone hears My voice and opens the door, I will come in to him."

Revelation 3:20

Perhaps it was the sudden death of my mother when I was only 10 years old that turned me into an argumentative, rebellious little boy.

Or perhaps it was that in the midst of a Muslim environment, we were Christians, and it troubled me privately that we had suffered so much trouble. Not only had we lost our mother, but also my father had to work very hard as a mason for very little pay. If we belonged to God, why did He not take better care of us — especially when we tried so hard!

My great-grandfather, Kanahia Lall, was one of the first in the Punjab (then a part of India) to accept Christ when the Presbyterian missionaries arrived with the gospel in the 1860's. As I looked at all the hardships my family was enduring, in contrast to the seemingly easy life of most people around us, I wondered what it was that had caused my great-grandfather to change his religion.

After completing my high school years, I went to Murray College in Sialkot. I became more and more proud, thinking that I knew everything. I used to listen to the missionaries, along with the Christian teachers and professors in all sorts of Bible classes and evangelistic meetings, but I was full of antagonism. I attended the meetings and classes simply to argue rather than to understand who Jesus Christ was and what Christianity was all about. It was a matter of great pride for me to enter into a discussion, force an argument and then win the argument. I thought that the more I argued, the better I was.

So I went to these missionaries to try to disturb them with my questions. I would ask, "Hasn't the Bible been changed?" Of course, many Muslims believe this. Always, with calmness and love, the missionaries responded to me by asking, "*Where* has the Bible been changed? Can you tell us?" Of course, I could not.

9

Then I would say, "You Christians believe in three gods, don't you? One, plus one, plus one — it equals three! Father, Son and Holy Spirit has to mean three gods!" Their answer was that I was using the wrong form of mathematics. Instead of adding and coming up with three gods, the equation was one, *times* one, *times* one — which equals *one*, not three.

"We believe in only one God," they explained, "but He manifests Himself in three different ways, while still being only one."

This made sense to me, but I would not admit that I understood. So I continued to argue with them about many of the questions that I had about the Bible. Sometimes I could see the truth in their answers, as well as in their kind and loving spirit as they spoke with me, but I did not want to give in and admit they were right.

Intrigued and Startled

But one fall evening in 1948 I was attending the annual Christian Convention in my city of Sialkot. These conventions and many others across Pakistan and India were founded at the turn of the century by John Hyde, a man of God whose honor and respect in that part of the world is reflected in his title, "Praying Hyde." Every year many thousands of nominal Christians as well as others would flock to these evangelistic meetings for a week or more.

As I sat there listening that evening to the speaker, I was intrigued by his clear explanation of the prophecies that foretold the crucifixion. Even more, I was startled by his assertion that Christ's death on the cross was for *me, personally*.

"He took *your* place on the cross," the man emphasized, repeating that it was because Jesus *loved me* that He had died for me. In all my years as a nominal Christian, I had never understood this truth before. God used this man of God to open my eyes and my heart, convicting me of my pride and waywardness and showing me that I needed the salvation that Jesus had provided for me. So when the speaker gave an invitation, I went forward with many others to confess and repent of my sin and receive Jesus Christ as my personal Savior.

As the minister counseled with me, I cried like a little baby for the way I had troubled Jesus Christ so much. My pride came tumbling down, because I knew that I had put Jesus on the cross so many times with my sins. This preacher showed me four verses of Scripture that night, and they seemed to come to life to me, even though I had heard them all before:

"For God so loved the world, that He gave His only begotten Son, that whoever believes in Him should not perish, but have eternal life" (John 3:16).

"For the wages of sin is death, but the free gift of God is eternal life in Christ Jesus our Lord" (Romans 6:23).

"But as many as received Him, to them He gave the right to become children of God, even to those who believe in His name" (John 1:12).

"Behold, I stand at the door and knock; if any one hears My voice and opens the door, I will come in to him, and will dine with him, and he with Me" (Revelation 3:20).

I asked Jesus to come into my heart, and He came in. It was so beautiful. Confessing and repenting of my sins, I simply asked Jesus to come into my heart, and He came in.

Zealous Joy

My heart really was filled with a new-found joy at that point, because I knew that I was a saved person. I began to want to read the Bible all the time, and I also found that I wanted to tell others who Jesus Christ is. I did everything I could to help accomplish this, especially giving out literature and distributing tracts.

Since I was quite young and bold, it wasn't long before I had become a very zealous preacher. At that time preaching on the street corners was allowed in Pakistan, so I often led evangelistic teams. We began by singing, with drums and a harmonium (a portable reed organ) as accompaniment, and a large crowd would gather. Then I would go and stand on a stone or something, and preach in a loud voice. A few people listened and received Christ as their Savior, even though I preached mostly about sin and God's judgment in a negative sort of way.

Even though at that time my one great desire in life was to tell the people around me about Jesus Christ, I realized that I was only skimming along on the surface. I was not really having the effectiveness that I longed for in my heart.

During those years, as I was finishing my college education, I was able to teach Urdu to some of the missionaries during my summer vacations. This was a double blessing for me, because in addition to earning enough money to keep me in school, I received much spiritual help from the missionaries.

So I listened carefully when one of these missionaries suggested to me that if I wanted to be able to preach with real power and authority, I should get some theological training. When he suggested that I go to the United States for this, I agreed that I was most willing and anxious to.

"But," I pointed out, "there are three difficulties that will have to be solved first, and they all have to do with money, which I don't have!" First, I needed money for my passage to the United States; next, I would need funds for my tuition for three years or more; and last, my living expenses would need to be provided for in some way.

"If God will provide these three things," I told my friend, "I am ready to go!"

An Ebenezer Experience

God did supply all these needs not long afterwards, and I found myself headed for California. It took nearly one month to get there, going by train to Karachi, flying to Hong Kong, taking a ship to San Francisco and then going by Greyhound bus down to Pasadena. When I arrived at Fuller Theological Seminary to begin my three years of training, I had $3.00 in my pocket and one change of clothing!

From that day on, the wonderful provision of the Lord never once faltered, as He faithfully provided my needs during those next three years. Much of His kind provision came through my dear "prayer mother," Ruby Wahlgren, and her husband, Russell Wahlgren, of Pasadena, who were my sponsors at Fuller.

Two months after my arrival I fell seriously ill, lying in a coma for three days at Los Angeles County Hospital. The doctors were mystified, finally concluding that I was dying of some fatal Asian disease. But a number of God's people at Fuller began to pray, and God chose to heal me in a miraculous way. I returned to my studies with a deep awareness that God had a special reason for sparing my life.

The miracles continued, happening so often that I felt like

Samuel, who set up a stone between Mizpah and Shen and named it Ebenezer (the Stone of Help), saying, "Hitherto hath the Lord helped us!" (I Samuel 7:12, KJV). How well I knew that none of this was my doing — it was the Lord's doing through His people to bring me there and keep me there.

Shortly after I had graduated from seminary and had been ordained as a minister of the gospel, a seminary friend named Gordon Klenck invited me to visit the headquarters of Campus Crusade for Christ, then located in Mound, Minnesota. Gordon and I had worked together with international students at UCLA our last year in seminary, and he had introduced me to Dr. Bill Bright, the president of Campus Crusade.

The Campus Crusade ministry was small then, with about 100 on the staff, but even so Bill Bright was becoming known as a leader in the Christian world. So I was very amazed, the day after I arrived in Mound, to see the president and founder of this growing student movement out working alongside his staff to put down sod grass on the lawn!

A Liberating Discovery

Later that day, during a rest break in the afternoon, Dr. Bright sat down with me on the grass and began to talk. As we shared together about spiritual things, he said frankly, "Kundan, I know that you have been to seminary, and now you are an ordained minister. You have all of the head-knowledge necessary for doing the Lord's work. But I want to ask you one thing: are you personally experiencing the filling of the Holy Spirit?"

"I know a lot about the Holy Spirit," I answered, "but to be honest with you, I don't think He is really working in my life right now."

In those days, neither the Four Spiritual Laws nor the Holy Spirit booklet had been printed, so Dr. Bright drew three circles on a piece of paper as he explained to me how I could be filled and empowered by the Holy Spirit. I was deeply impressed when he said, "To be filled with the Holy Spirit is to be filled with Jesus Christ Himself." I had never heard this before. We prayed together on the grass that afternoon, and I learned what it really means to appropriate the power of the Holy Spirit in my daily life (See Appendix III).

This new, clear understanding of the ministry of the Holy

Spirit in my life meant very much to me. The wonderful discovery of how to breathe spiritually and walk in the power and fullness of the Holy Spirit was so liberating it was like opening a door into a whole new way of life, particularly in relation to my witness for Jesus Christ. I realized that my job is simply to share the gospel, with the responsibility of convicting and converting others left to the Holy Spirit Himself. As I participated in the Campus Crusade training in evangelism there in Mound, I saw that this was the definition of true evangelism: we share the truth about Jesus Christ in the power of the Holy Spirit, and then we leave the results to God.

Personal Intentions Reversed

After several weeks of training at Mound, Dr. Bright shared with all of us one night his vision to see the Great Commission fulfilled around the world through the national believers of every country. Afterwards he talked with me personally, challenging me to pray about going back to Pakistan to begin the Campus Crusade ministry there.

But at that point, I had no intention of ever returning to minister in Pakistan. For one thing, I liked the comfortable way of life I had enjoyed in the United States, and it was wonderful to have so many personal advantages and so much more freedom to minister. And also, the idea of going back and talking to Muslims about Jesus Christ seemed impossible to me. "I can't do that," I thought to myself. "They are so hard. It's not like here in America, where so many people are ready to hear about Jesus and to respond to His love. Back home, they won't even listen to me!"

However, I did agree to pray about it, and the Holy Spirit began to convict me and convince me. "Only nationals can reach nationals," Dr. Bright had emphasized, and his statement repeated itself over and over in my mind. "Only a Pakistani like you can really reach other Pakistanis and disciple them for Christ," he had continued. "It's going to take national believers like you, who are not only trained and committed, but who are also filled and empowered by the Holy Spirit, to saturate Pakistan with the love of Christ."

After about three weeks, I went to Dr. Bright and told him that God had given me the necessary courage and peace to accept his challenge. On our knees, we claimed together the promise of Jeremiah 33:3, which was to become one of the pillars of my life and ministry in the Middle East: "Call unto Me, and I will answer thee, and show thee great and mighty things, which thou knowest not" (KJV).

I was really overwhelmed at the thought of accepting this heavy responsibility. After Korea, Pakistan would be Campus Crusade's second overseas ministry. I knew how limited my own strength and wisdom were, but I was willing to be used — and I had been convinced through Campus Crusade's training that reaching Pakistan was the Holy Spirit's job, and my job was only to make myself totally available to the Holy Spirit!

Even so, I was feeling the weight of this new challenge as I prepared to return to my homeland at the end of 1959. Dr. Bright's parting talk with me at the airport as I left was a timely reminder.

"Kundan," he said, "remember that *you* are not going to win Muslims for Christ back in Pakistan."

I was shocked for a moment, and I asked, "No? Why not?"

"Because," Dr. Bright reminded me, "the *Holy Spirit* is going to do that."

I smiled in relief, and my anxiety over beginning a "successful" ministry melted into anticipation to see what God was going to do.

Simple but Powerful Format

Soon after my arrival back home in Pakistan, the Lord led me to certain influential Christian men who were willing to form an Advisory Board registered as Pakistan Campus Crusade for Christ. As a result, early in 1960, I began going out to speak about the Lord Jesus Christ wherever any opportunity was given — in large cities or small villages, on campuses, in churches and in communities.

When I explained the gospel and gave invitations, many people came to know Jesus Christ as their personal Savior, and everywhere many lives were touched, especially among the young people. Basically, I just followed the simple, clear format of the Four Spiritual Laws (See Appendix II). I could see that it was important to stress the love of God before going into the sinfulness of man. And after I had explained the uniqueness of Jesus as the only way to God, I was careful always to give people an opportunity to receive Christ.

In my hometown of Sialkot, a great number of young people came to hear about God's love and forgiveness made known through Christ for them, and it was here that the Lord drew Iqbal Chaudhry and me together. She was also from a nominal Christian family, but she had been hungering for the reality of a spiritual life that was deep and alive.

Conversion in a Convent

On one of my visits to the mountain town of Murree, I learned that Miss Chaudhry was teaching in a nearby convent school. Little did I realize, when I asked her to make tea one afternoon for the boys who attended my College Life meeting, that just three weeks before she had abruptly stopped taking instruction to become a Roman Catholic nun! Confused and restless, she had vowed to give no more time or thought to religion.

As I gave my College Life talk that afternoon, I spoke from John 3. Although I was unaware of it, Iqbal had become so curious to hear my message that she finally pried open the kitchen window so that she could hear!

When I escorted her back to the convent afterwards, she tried, in an offhand manner, to ask several questions about my message. Realizing that her heart was open to spiritual things, I repeated my explanation of how to receive Christ, asking if she would like to invite Him into her life. She hurriedly denied any personal interest, so I said goodbye and left her.

Later I learned that when she returned to her convent room, she could neither eat nor rest nor sleep. After many hours of struggling, she knelt by her bed, well after midnight, to invite Christ into her heart "just like that preacher said." The following morning, the entire convent was snickering over reports that Iqbal had awakened her Muslim friend across the hall in the middle of the night to announce, "I have just invited Christ into my heart, and He came in!" The sleepy teacher had peered back at her in a daze, finally concluding, "Iqbal, you have had a bad dream! Just go back to bed, and you will be all right in the morning!"

Iqbal was most happy to acknowledge the rumors, and by the end of that school term, every nun, teacher and pupil in the convent knew that something wonderful had happened to Miss Chaudhry, who claimed to have "become" a Christian.

She began to grow quickly in the Lord, and soon we realized that the Lord had a special work for us to do — together! By the end of that year, with the blessings of our two families, we had become man and wife. I have not stopped thanking God over the years for blessing me with such a capable helpmeet in God's work. Most of all, she is a woman of prayer who stands with me in every demand of our ministry.

Revolutionary Truths

Our new ministry in Pakistan continued to grow, and many gave their lives to Jesus when they learned the simple truth of God's love. When I saw that the presentation of the gospel through the Four Spiritual Laws was so effective among my people, I translated this little booklet into our national language of Urdu and began to teach the young people and others how to share the love of God.

At the same time, I was explaining to as many as possible the wonderful discovery of the Spirit-filled life. As they experienced a newly abundant life, they began to see real, lasting fruit through their witness for Christ. I could see that the Holy Spirit booklet was equally important as a tool in equipping the believers in Pakistan to live and share the abundant Christian life, so I also translated and printed this booklet in Urdu.

I was greatly humbled, as a young man beginning a new ministry in my country, to realize that the whole concept of the Spirit-filled life, which had been so new and revolutionary in my own life, was just as wonderful and effective among my fellow national believers in Pakistan — whether laymen, young people or even clergymen.

One day the well-known pastor of a local church came to talk with me. In great discouragement he confessed, "You have been back in Pakistan only a very short time now, and yet people have thronged to learn more from you, and their Christian lives have come to life in a wonderful way."

Shaking his head, he continued, "I see such a difference between your work and mine. You are very young, just out of seminary, and I have been a pastor for a great many years. I have worked hard, preaching and visiting people, but attendance at my church is dropping off, and hardly any of the members seem to be growing spiritually. Where have I failed?" he asked despondently.

What a joyous privilege it was for me to pass on to this dear pastor the secret of the Spirit-filled life, just as Dr. Bill Bright had shared it with me a few years before.

"This is amazing," he remarked to me, as together we went over the Holy Spirit booklet, which was then in mimeographed form. "For all these years I have been preaching about the Holy Spirit, and yet I have never understood this simple truth before! But now I know how to be sure that I am filled with the Holy Spirit, and I understand about this 'spiritual breathing,' too."

From that day on, this pastor's pulpit ministry was transformed. Church attendance began to increase so steadily that within the next year, the church was forced to add an extension to make space for all the people who were coming.

I have never forgotten this "object lesson" which occurred early in my ministry. To me it demonstrated the dynamic power that is released once any believer understands how to be filled with the Holy Spirit and begins to walk in the Spirit as a way of life.

Also, it indicated that not only did young students and untaught lay people need such training, but also that pastors and Christian workers were hungry for this vital training, too — training to help equip them to live Spirit-filled Christian lives and to share the positive truths of the gospel of Christ in an effective, fruitful way.

The kernel of that concept was to remain in my mind and become the central purpose of a strategic gathering to be held many years after I had left Pakistan . . .

CHAPTER THREE

Magnet in the Mideast

*"Thou hast enclosed me behind and before, and laid Thy
hand upon me."*

Psalm 139:5

After the first year or so of ministry in Pakistan, I was
tempted to start doing something other than focus on training
with students, laymen and pastors. After a steady succession
of training conferences and teaching sessions — Leadership
Training Institutes, summer camps, Lay Institutes for Evangelism and the like — I became tired of teaching the same basic
truths over and over again. Yet at every training opportunity,
the Pakistani Christians continued to thank me for sharing
these "new truths" with them. The Holy Spirit used this to
keep the focus of my ministry upon training.

I finally realized that this was the most important thing I
could do for the believers in Pakistan. First they needed to
understand the basic truths of the gospel for themselves, and
then they needed to know how to share those truths in a clear
way with others. After that, in order for them to experience
abundant Christian lives and to want to be daily witnesses for
Christ, they also needed to know how to breathe spiritually,
appropriating the filling and control of the Holy Spirit as a way
of life.

So week after week, I gave myself to teaching and training,
passing on to my new staff as well as to hundreds of others the
same simple principles which had brought such a change to
my own life. My schedule became very busy, and in the process the number of obstacles and difficulties for the ministry
seemed to multiply. I was particularly thankful for God's timing at that point in bringing Dr. Bright to visit me in Pakistan.
He demonstrated to me by example a concept which I began to
apply in every crisis I faced after that.

Stranded on the Border

I had gone to the Wagha border between Lahore and New

Delhi to meet Dr. Bright, who was traveling from India to see me for three days. He was scheduled to address the annual meeting of the entire Christian leadership of Lahore, Pakistan. However, after Dr. Bright had already cleared his passport through the Indian immigration officials and walked across "no man's land" to the Pakistani section, he discovered that his travel agent had somehow failed to secure a Pakistani visa for him! He had just canceled out his single-entry Indian visa, and with the political tension between India and Pakistan at that time, no Pakistani border official would dare to grant him a visa on the spot without proper clearances.

So there stood Dr. Bright, stranded in "no man's land" — and to make it even more complicated, it was a holiday, so government offices were closed! I managed to get permission to walk out and talk with Dr. Bright, and I was stunned when he explained the situation.

As we stood there looking at each other in "no man's land," Dr. Bright said to me, "Kundan, let's pray."

That seemed like a good idea to me, so we bowed our heads right there in the presence of the Lord and the border policemen.

"Lord Jesus," Dr. Bright prayed, "thank You for bringing me here. I praise Your name for this situation. Amen."

I raised my head and stared at him. In my heart I was saying, "What kind of a man is this? He didn't even ask God for a visa! He just praised Him!"

Then I watched God answer Dr. Bright's prayer of praise. He turned to a border policeman, asking for the telephone number of the top security official.

"He is not in his office, because today is a holiday," explained the policeman.

"Then give me his home telephone number, please," Dr. Bright asked. Within a few minutes, Dr. Bright was explaining his dilemma to the top official, who then spoke to the border police, instructing them to let Dr. Bright enter Pakistan. This is still one of the most amazing miracles I ever saw — Dr. Bright was allowed to spend three days in Pakistan without ever being issued a visa!

And so I learned my lesson: whatever happens, praise God. Since that time, I have, in obedience and as an act of faith, bowed my head hundreds of times to say, "Thank You, Lord. I praise Your name for this situation." I often repeat two verses either aloud or in my heart: "And we know that God causes all things to work together for good to those who love God, to those who are called according to His purpose" (Romans 8:28); "In everything give thanks; for this is God's will for you in Christ Jesus" (I Thessalonians 5:18).

And it works! This wonderful, amazing power in praising God has been a great bulwark to me in serving the Lord Jesus Christ through all the difficulties of ministry in the Middle East.

A Ph.D. vs. the Great Commission

After eight years as the director of Pakistan Campus Crusade, I took my wife and small son, Shalem, with me for an interim period of further education in the United States. Taking a teaching position to support us, I began to work toward earning my Ph.D. in education, which was a personal goal I had cherished for some time. In the process, we bought a nice home in Covina, Calif., and I was considering taking a pastorate and settling down in America. Our application for naturalization had been accepted, and our son was just getting started in the primary grades of a fine Christian school.

But one day Bill and Vonette Bright called us, and they asked my wife and me to come see them. As soon as we could arrange a time, we went to their home, and there Dr. Bright made an observation that I already knew in my heart: "Kundan, you don't need that Ph.D. You already have a wonderful education. And you also have a great deal of experience in ministering among Muslims."

"He's absolutely right," I thought to myself.

Then he continued, "Kundan, Muslims are lost without Jesus Christ, and *you* are the kind of man God can use in a mighty way to proclaim His love to them."

As always, Dr. Bright's sensitivity to the leading of the Holy Spirit had a wonderful influence in my life. I responded, "You are right, Bill. I don't need that Ph.D. I need to get busy once again in the task of reaching the unreached — especially the Muslims!"

So for the next two years I served as a traveling representative in the United States for the International Student Ministry, a special thrust of Campus Crusade to help reach the "mission field" of internationals studying in American colleges and universities. In this capacity I visited nearly every state from Hawaii to New York — speaking on campuses and at free speech rallies, interacting with students from Hindu, Buddhist and Muslim backgrounds, and challenging American Christians to get involved in reaching international students for Jesus Christ. I saw with fresh understanding just how hungry the hearts of these students were for the love and forgiveness of God, and during this time I saw many students from various religious backgrounds come to know Jesus as their Savior. It was then that I realized that I would never be content until every hungry heart around the world had a clear opportunity to hear about and experience Christ's love.

Move to Manila

So when our Asian director of affairs, Bailey Marks, challenged me to move my family to the Philippines in 1973 and become his traveling representative in Central Asia and the Middle East, my heart was prepared. We sold our home, packed up our belongings for the eleventh time since our marriage and moved across the ocean to Manila.

What a joy it was to have a personal part in locating and recruiting the first national staff couples for our ministries in Nepal, Iran, Burma and Bangladesh — and then to see them come to Manila for several months of training in spiritual multiplication. Even while I was challenging them to consider God's calling to join our ministry, I found myself repeating the words of Dr. Bright that had been burned into my heart many years before: "Nationals are the best people to reach nationals."

As I traveled from country to country, experiencing wonderful miracles and answers to prayer, the Lord gave me much more of a burden for the Muslim world than I had ever experienced before. Sometimes I was moved to tears as I realized how many people in the Middle East had not even heard the name of Jesus Christ — like in my homeland of Pakistan, where 80% of the population is illiterate.

But in spite of my growing love and compassion for the Muslim world in particular, I was not prepared for the challenge that Dr. Bright offered me one snowy night in February,

1975. The international leaders of the Campus Crusade ministry had been meeting in Munich, Germany, and I was asked to meet with Dr. Bright after the evening sessions. It was well after midnight before our appointment began.

Dr. Bright started by saying, "I want you to consider taking a responsibility much greater than you have ever had before." Then he walked over to the world map on the wall, tracing with his finger the area from Pakistan across the Arab nations over to Morocco.

"I want you to open up the Middle East as a new area of affairs in the Campus Crusade ministry," he said. "God has given me peace that you are the man for the Middle East — one of the last virtually unreached regions of the world. So I want you to pray about this overnight, and let me know your decision in the morning."

I was almost numb, and I could hardly speak. I was overwhelmed with a sense of unworthiness. But before I left that night, Dr. Bright asked me to pray with him over the map. So we laid our hands over that map, claiming the entire Muslim world for God through the love of Jesus Christ. For more than half an hour we prayed, with tears, and when we had finished it seemed that peace had fallen upon me like a dew from the Holy Spirit. I spent the rest of that night alone with God, and the next morning I accepted Dr. Bright's appointment as director of Middle East affairs.

The following evening, Dr. Bright announced my new appointment to the other directors of affairs, representing Europe, Asia, Latin America, Africa and North America. And then he did an unusual thing: he asked me to kneel, and as he and the other directors placed their hands on my head and shoulders, they prayed and commissioned me for this task. It was one of the most moving experiences of my life, and all of us wept as we sensed the Holy Spirit confirming my call back to the Middle East.

My brothers in the Lord who were with me in that room knew that the future would not be easy for me. They knew that optimism and wonderful plans and hard work could never bring about the fulfillment of the Great Commission in the Middle East. But together with me that evening, they *believed God* for the supernatural working of His Holy Spirit to sweep across the Middle East and the Muslim world. That faith and love, built on mutual respect and trust that knows no race or nationality, still touches my deepest being and rejoices my heart.

Wars and Rumors of War

When I began my new responsibilities to direct the ministry of Campus Crusade in the Middle East in July of 1975, it seemed logical to set up my continental headquarters in Beirut, Lebanon, which was the acknowledged center of Christian activity and missions for most of the Middle East. However, the Lebanese civil war intervened, and two days before my family and I planned to leave for Beirut, the national director of our Lebanon ministry telephoned and advised me not to come. Within two weeks Beirut was ablaze, engulfed in full-scale war.

After a few weeks, I made a quick trip alone to visit the staff in our two other established national ministries — Pakistan and Iran. After much prayer and consultation, I decided to locate our new Middle East Office in Tehran, Iran. At that time, every knowledgeable expert assured us that Iran, of all the countries in the Middle East, could be expected to remain stable for many years to come.

So in early January of 1976 we flew into a snowy Tehran, where we were to establish our continental headquarters over the next three years. At that time, our staff was small in number — just my family, one Iranian staff couple and my secretary. But Iran provided a good location as I moved about the Middle East, and communication facilities with our staff in other nations were reliable. Within just two and a half years, our staff family in Tehran numbered 19, including a team of teachers with The *Agape* Movement — a specialized ministry within Campus Crusade that enables Christians to minister for Christ in other countries through their professional skills and vocations.

But when it became apparent that problems in Iran were building toward a violent change, all of our western staff were forced to evacuate by early January of 1979. Since the *Agape* Movement teachers' primary school closed its doors, they returned to the United States. Our administrative staff transferred to the island of Cyprus — the same island where we had evacuated some other "western staff refugees" from the Lebanese civil war.

My family and I stayed on in Tehran with our national staff as long as we could. It was not that we were not frightened at times, because our hearts froze the first time we heard the loud, wailing chant of "Allah-hu-Akbar" (meaning "God is great!") sweep across the darkened capital of Tehran at curfew hour. The electricity was cut off, people shouted angrily from the rooftops at the soldiers and tanks in the streets, and from every direction came the sound of machine gun fire. News broadcasts on radio and television had been abandoned for days, and all the newspapers were shut down as well.

Standing in Line by Faith

But when this happened night after night, we became almost accustomed to the disturbances. We spent the bulk of our time on our knees, praying and reading God's Word together. My teenage son and I spent most of our remaining time standing in lines for hours every day, trying to get rationed amounts of bread, bottled gas, kerosene and gasoline.

Finally, in early February our national director in Iran told me, "Brother, I think you must leave. Even though you are from Pakistan, people look at you as a foreigner. It would be better for your family in these days, when we cannot say what will happen, if you leave for a while." I knew that he was right — the day before, our son, Shalem, had been refused bread with the curt remark, "No bread for the foreigners!" The same thing had happened when I pled with the delivery man for furnace heating oil. He shouted, "Nothing for the foreigners! Go away from here!" and drove off down the street.

So, although we had sincerely identified with our national staff and wanted to stay with them as long as the Lord permitted, we hurriedly packed and made ready to go — only to learn that the airport had closed! And even worse, our home was only blocks away from the headquarters of Savak, the hated secret police, and we had seen the armed mobs gathering for a deadly attack. By God's grace, just two hours before the street was barricaded, we escaped from our house to another part of the city, taking refuge in the home of a Christian brother. For more than a week, we lived with agonizing tension. The skies were black with smoke, and the streets were filled with students and even children armed with guns and hand grenades. Then came the announcement over radio and TV that the city's tap water had been poisoned, and we could not even drink the water.

During those last few days, we trembled to see more of war and hate than we had ever experienced. But God was gracious to us hour by hour, and we were awed by His daily protection of our lives and His loving care of even our thoughts and emotions.

Finally, a few days after Ayatollah Khomeini's triumphant return to Iran, we stood in line for hours at Tehran's Mehrabad Airport to board a flight for Karachi, Pakistan. Two days later, we were reunited with our staff team in Cyprus.

Facing the Future by Faith

I recall a number of dramatic experiences through my years of ministry in the Middle East, but none was quite like the months of tension and chaos in Tehran. Even so, I have come to thank God for all that He taught me as I shared this harrowing experience with our Iranian staff. In a very real sense, I know that God's Word is dramatically true when it cautions, "You do not know what your life will be like tomorrow" (James 4:14).

We have now relocated the headquarters of our Middle East ministry, known as Lifeagape International of the Middle East, on the pleasant little island of Cyprus. It is wonderful to be living in a Christian country, one that is so centrally located in the Middle East. Cyprus is such an interesting mixture of European and Arab cultures, and I am most thankful for the reasonable cost of living as well as excellent connections for travel and communications.

However, after Iran, I am very much aware that I do not know what will happen tomorrow — even though my heart and mind are filled with plans and prayers for the future. Just five years ago, this calm island was wracked by war between Turkish and Greek Cypriots, and now an ominous Green Line separating the two is drawn across the island, policed by United Nations troops. Every time I drive to the capital city of Nicosia and see that barricaded Green Line, I am reminded that apart from the Prince of Peace, there is no hope for peace anywhere in the Middle East.

But, significantly, because God is sovereign, I found myself living in Cyprus — the very place that God had impressed me to choose months earlier for a gathering we were to call the Middle East Leadership Fellowship . . .

CHAPTER
FOUR

Quest for Atonement

"[Christ] . . . offered one sacrifice for sins for all time."
Hebrews 10:12

It was during those three years in Iran that I began to think through my years of ministry and interaction with Middle Easterners, particularly those of Muslim background.

Certainly the Muslim world represented one of the world's most sizeable and resistant blocs of "unreached peoples" over the centuries. Internationally, there were now 720 million Muslims — one out of every six human beings in the world! Nearly 60 nations claimed to be Islamic, and another 150 countries had at least some Muslim population.

I knew that I was not the first one to have discovered, through a long progression of experiences both positive and mistaken, that I could not convert a Muslim. I had learned a great deal about Islam, both because I had studied it carefully and because I had grown up in an Islamic country. Through the years, I had come to understand the convictions of devout Muslims, as well as the common beliefs and practices of the masses of nominal Muslims.

Because of my knowledge of Islam and my training in Christian apologetics, I could usually convince a Muslim, at least intellectually, of the basic truths of Christianity. Whenever that happened, however, he inevitably became *my* convert, rather than Jesus' convert, and eventually he dropped away.

I knew that the difference lay in the work of the Holy Spirit: when the Spirit convicts and convinces a Muslim, he will be truly converted, submitting his life permanently to the Lord Jesus Christ. So I decided when I came back to minister in the Muslim world that I wanted genuine converts — Jesus' converts.

Love Communicates

Since that time, I have seen Muslims come to know and love Christ in a vital, personal way many times — first in Pakistan, and then in many different countries. I have not always made sense to them, most probably, and I haven't always explained some of the theological truths about Jesus very well. Nevertheless, because the Holy Spirit was working, the reality of Christ's love pierced their hearts.

The more I shared the revolutionary, unconditional love of God with people in the Middle East, the more confident I became that God's Word is living, powerful and authoritative. I am a firm believer in quoting Scripture as I witness for Jesus Christ. For one thing, I find that when I am quoting the words of Jesus all the time, I cannot help loving the people with whom I am sharing!

So I learned by experience not to depend upon knowledge of argumentative logic to convince another Middle Easterner that Jesus Christ is the only, unique way to God. Rather, I learned to rely upon the filling and empowering of the Holy Spirit, Who is always faithful to communicate the Word of God and the love of Christ to others through me.

This does not mean that I think it is not important to share an intelligent, clear answer to the frequent objections and questions which are in the minds of Muslims. They deserve to hear logical answers to their honest questions. It is vital that we clarify the Christian faith to them, but we must do so with love and understanding.

One of the most helpful guidelines to me concerning this has been the wise counsel of I Peter 3:15, which says, "But sanctify Christ as Lord in your hearts, always being ready to make a defense to every one who asks you to give an account for the hope that is in you, *yet with gentleness and reverence*." By following this principle, I have avoided arguments so that every discussion can center around Jesus and His uniqueness.

A Devout Young Man

One of the first of Jesus' converts in Pakistan through my ministry was a devout young man whom I will call Akbar. When I first met him, he was enrolled in an Islamic seminary, preparing to become a Muslim missionary.

My contact with Akbar came through some of our Christian students who were attending one of our summer camps in Murree, up in the mountains of Pakistan. Every summer, we sponsored several weeks of spiritual camps in this mountain retreat area. Our meetings drew many young people and even lay men and women. Not only did these sessions provide an escape from the scorching heat down on the plains, but they also enabled us to share with interested Christians some practical training in how to experience the abundant Christian life — and then how to share the love of Christ with others.

One afternoon some of our students had approached Akbar while they were in the town sharing Christ's love with people on the street. Interrupting their presentation of the Four Spiritual Laws, Akbar began to ask them many penetrating questions which they did not know how to answer. Admitting their limited understanding of theological questions, they responded, "If you really want answers to these questions, come back with us and ask them of our camp director, Mr. Massey."

So Akbar came, and that evening at the camp site, I presented a message on the uniqueness of Jesus Christ, explaining in detail why He alone could provide atonement for our sins. Akbar was familiar with the concept of man's inherent sinfulness, but he listened in amazement as I reviewed how God's demand for a sinless sacrifice had been met perfectly by Christ, the Lamb of God.

My message was not very eloquent — in fact, it was quite simple, but because I explained every point upon the authority of God's Word, the Holy Spirit gave it power. The Bible is still sharper than any two-edged sword, and the Holy Spirit uses it powerfully when our mere human arguments could not possibly succeed.

Counting the Cost

That night, Akbar's heart was touched. On the surface he appeared to have come to argue, but in reality he was fascinated by these new truths he was hearing. He had planned to return to the town after a few hours, but instead he stayed on at our camp for three days. Finally, he came to me and announced, "I want to accept Jesus Christ as my personal Savior."

I was reluctant to encourage him. In fact, I warned him of the consequences he could expect from such a decision.

"You are an only son," I reminded him. "Your family will cast you out and disinherit you. Instead of being respected back in your community, you will be despised, even hated and perhaps attacked." I urged him to think long and hard about such ugly consequences, to truly "count the cost" before making any decision.

But Akbar just smiled and repeated, "I want to accept Jesus Christ." Then he proceeded to explain to me why he wanted to make such a radical about-face, from Muslim missionary to Christian believer.

"All my life," he said, "I have been taught to believe that sin is more powerful than man, and that it is impossible for man to conquer sin.

"Our sacred book, the Qur'an, teaches us that we must earn our salvation through good works, because at the end of our lives God will weigh all our good deeds against our bad ones. That is why the Qur'an talks about sin so much, and urges us to do as much good as possible so we will be sure to outweigh all our bad deeds."

He explained that in his theological studies he had found at least 15 different Arabic words used in the Qur'an to denote the various types of sin. They included everything from mischief and "straying" to premeditated evil and depravity — all of which required the forgiveness of Allah.

Then he mentioned that the Qur'an indicates that even Muhammad himself needed forgiveness, because it states in Surah 48, *Al-Fath*, Victory: :1,2, "Lo, we have given thee (O Muhammad) a signal victory that Allah may forgive thee of thy sin which is past, and that which is to come."

As a seminary student, Akbar told me he had heard several explanations on the meaning of this verse from famous Muslim commentators. Ibn Hisham, for example, quoting Muhammad Ibn Ishaq, wrote that when Muhammad was a little boy, two beings robed in white met him one day. They were carrying a golden bowl full of snow. They removed his heart, extracted a dark clot of sin from it, washed it in snow, and then returned it.

"When I read this story," Akbar related, "I sincerely wished that some good angels robed in white could come with a bowlful of snow and wash my heart clean, too!"

Desperate Condition

He told me that the more he read the Qur'an and the Hadith and other sources of Islamic belief, the more conscious he became of his own burden of sin.

"One night I was lying in bed thinking about the story of Adam in the Garden of Eden," he related. "I had been consoling myself that even though I had many sins, all of my good works would cancel them out, according to the surah in the Qur'an which says, 'Whoso keepeth his duty to Allah, He will remit from him his evil deeds' (Surah 65, *At-Talaq*, Divorce: 5). But then it suddenly occurred to me that God punished Adam very severely for only one sin, and threw him out of Eden. Adam, I saw, was not able to restore his fellowship with God by just doing two good works to cancel out his one sin!"

I nodded in agreement, amazed at Akbar's perception.

"So I became quite alarmed," Akbar continued, "because I thought how much Adam suffered for just one sin — and imagine how many sins I have committed! Fortunately, I thought, at least I had never committed any of the three unpardonable sins — apostasy, polytheism *(shirk)* or killing a believer. But I had noted that all through the Qur'an even the prophets confessed their sins and sought God's forgiveness. No one could escape!

"I prayed that night that somehow God would relieve me of this desperate condition and give me comfort. But no comfort came."

Search for an Intercessor

So Akbar told himself, "Surely the prophet Muhammed will be my intercessor." But, to his dismay, he soon found a verse in the Qur'an in which Muhammad said, "Nor know I what will be done with me or with you." And in one Hadith, the prophet Muhammad even told his beloved daughter, Fatima: "You may ask me anything, but I cannot save you from God's wrath."

Confused but still searching, Akbar began to wonder whether he was following the right way after all.

"One day as I was offering my prayers," he said, "I began to ask God to show me His true way. I had read something that I could not forget about Christ, calling Him the intercessor in this world and the world to come. I knew that I needed an intercessor, and the prophet Muhammad clearly admitted that he was not that intercessor."

He went on to explain that Islam teaches that Jesus was a great prophet, so he had already learned something about Jesus in his seminary studies.

"But as I listened to you teach that first night," he admitted, "I saw for the first time the supernatural aspects of Jesus' life and ministry on earth. His virgin birth according to prophecy, His sinless life, His miracles, His unique teachings, His substitutionary death, His bodily resurrection, His promise of coming again . . . I can only come to one conclusion: Jesus was Himself God, and He alone can forgive my sins."

Convinced by all this of the sincerity and depth of Akbar's commitment to Jesus Christ, I shared the Four Spiritual Laws with him. He nodded carefully as I went over each point slowly to be sure that he understood it all, step by step, before he bowed to pray a simple prayer:

> "Lord Jesus, I need You. Thank You for dying on the cross for my sins. I confess and repent of my sins, and I open the door of my life and receive You as my Savior and Lord. Thank You for forgiving my sins. Take control of the throne of my life. Make me the kind of person You want me to be. Amen."

Once he became a new creature in Christ, Akbar bravely dropped his given name and took a Christian name in its place, thus announcing his new profession of faith. As we had expected, this faith was tested immediately.

Disowned and Tried

Upon his return home, he first shared his decision with his parents. In great embarrassment and rage, they threw him out of their home and disowned him. They even took away his young wife and told everyone that their son had become mentally unbalanced.

Akbar had expected such a response, for from his childhood his parents had taught him to react in the same way toward anyone who would dare to abandon the Islamic faith.

But then his family, determined to defame his character and even to call for his death, went to some local officials to report his defection to Christianity. Accusing their son of stealing money and jewelry from them and then running away to join a Christian camp, they branded him a thief and a traitor who deserved the death penalty.

However, at that time there were many young people from our camps and other believers all over Pakistan who were praying for Akbar, and the Lord did a mighty miracle in answer to their prayers. We learned later that it so happened that the judge presiding over Akbar's trial in his hometown had a close friend who knew the truth about Akbar's situation. When the judge learned that the parents were putting forth false charges against their son, he decided the case in Akbar's favor!

Even more to magnify the miracle, the judge also issued a warning to Akbar's parents when he handed down his decision: "I warn you," he cautioned them, "do not kill Akbar, or try to have him killed, because if you do, I will hold you personally responsible for his murder, and your own lives will be forfeited." His parents were furious, of course, but their hands had been stopped by their own authorities.

Over the years, Akbar's father and his other relatives have refused to forgive Akbar or even speak to him, much to his sorrow. But a few years ago, as his mother lay dying, she begged to see her only son again. The family denied her request, threatening that they would not even hold a proper funeral for her if she mentioned Akbar's name again. Akbar finally learned of her death indirectly, and when he tried to show his respect by attending her funeral, his relatives insulted him and threw him out of the funeral ceremonies.

Despite this persecution from his family, as well as from others who were angered to learn that he had changed his faith, Akbar remained faithful to his Savior and Lord and grew steadily in Christ. After he graduated from a Bible school, God gave him a wonderful Christian wife, and together they are seeing much fruit from their ministry of evangelism and discipleship for Christ in Pakistan.

God's Forgiveness Is Free

As I thought back on Akbar's conversion, I marveled that he had come to Christ in such a short period of time, even though he was a devout Muslim. So I began to wonder: what aspect of the Christian faith was used in particular by the Holy Spirit to cause him to turn with his whole heart to Jesus Christ? I thought over all of our times of interaction together before he invited Christ into his life, and one strong impression stood out.

Perhaps the most overwhelming truth to Akbar was his amazed discovery that God has *already provided* for his forgiveness and salvation — that these were free gifts! In fact, the only reason that Akbar did not receive Christ that first evening he heard me speak was because he could not comprehend that God would love him so much that He would actually pay for Akbar's sins Himself.

Salvation by faith rather than through good works was an astonishing concept to Akbar, because for years he had been trying to attain forgiveness of his sins by doing good deeds — fasting, giving alms, reading and memorizing the Qur'an, repeating the creed, and so on.

Yet, in spite of all that, Akbar was still filled with dread whenever he thought of the day of final reckoning before Allah. According to the Imam ar Rezi, he believed that on the Day of Judgment "Allah will set up a balance with two scales . . . on which He will weigh the deeds of mankind, good or evil." He had read the assurances of Ibn Abbas, who wrote, "The believer's deeds will be the best. On the scales, his good deeds will outweigh his ill deeds." But no matter how hard Akbar tried to earn his forgiveness with his good works, he was still burdened with a sense of his sins and guilt.

I could see that Akbar's dilemma was the same one facing people all over the Middle East, from all of the world's major religions: men are trying to reach God by their own good works. But the unique truth of Christianity proclaims that it is *God* who is seeking men! He is offering them a free pardon from their sins, a pardon which He Himself has purchased through the shed blood of His perfect Lamb, the Lord Jesus Christ.

It is this simple truth which we believers in the Middle East must lovingly offer to those around us who are trying so very sincerely and desperately to please God. I wondered, how many of my fellow believers in the Muslim world knew how to share this simple, positive concept with their friends and neighbors? I wished that I could somehow have even half an hour with all of them to share with them how to communicate this love with those who know Him not . . .

CHAPTER
FIVE

The Essential Sacrifice

"But God demonstrates His own love toward us, in that
while we were yet sinners, Christ died for us."

Romans 5:8

When we observed our first Easter in Tehran, in the spring of 1976, my mind was flooded with memories. It had been several years since I had celebrated the resurrection of Christ in a typically Middle Eastern setting, where we follow the traditional custom of visiting our neighbors and friends on the occasion of their religious holidays.

Several families and acquaintances came to call on us, to acknowledge our Easter celebration — just as we had gone to their homes a few weeks before to take them food and sweets in observance of their Persian New Year, which falls in late March. What a perfect opportunity such a custom offers for the believer who is prepared to share the true meaning and significance of Easter! I recalled the many times during my ministry in Pakistan when we had used this tradition to such advantage during the Christmas and Easter seasons.

My mind went back to one unforgettable incident in Pakistan just before Easter one year, when I had access to the classic Christian film, "King of Kings." All that spring I had scheduled showings in the villages surrounding the city where we lived. In most of these rural settings, I was able to find several Christian families who would agree to provide a place for an evening showing, usually in an open space outside their homes.

Village Film Showing

One evening I set out early with a young companion, a first-year college student. We arrived at the village in plenty of time to set up our projector, hook up its portable generator, stretch a sheet across a nearby wall for a screen, and then help spread out straw mats on the ground for our expected audience.

35

Word spread quickly among the villagers that someone had come to show a film. As evening turned from dusk to darkness, many saw the bright lights and came to find out what was happening. Then the Christians in the village began to sing from the *Zabur* (Psalms of David), accompanied by the drums and harmonium, so that even more villagers were attracted by the commotion. It wasn't long until we had run out of mats for them to sit on, and several thousand had to sit on the ground.

I estimated that at least 10,000 finally had gathered — adults, teenagers, children and even the elderly of the village — by the time I turned on the projector. Since the film was in English, I talked into a loudspeaker as the movie went along, doing the narration in Urdu, our national language.

Everyone remained quiet and absorbed in the film until we neared the end, which shows where Jesus was brought to trial. I began to sense a growing restlessness that was stirring across the crowd. I had come to expect this, because most Muslims cannot accept the fact that Jesus, whom they honor as a great prophet, could actually have been crucified. They have been taught to believe that God loved Jesus so much that He would not allow Him to suffer such a terrible death. Instead, God provided another man who looked like Jesus for the Jews to crucify, while Jesus Himself was lifted up to heaven (Surah 4, *An-Nisa*, Women: 156-158).

Unique Message of the Cross

Sensing a current of antagonism in the audience, I stopped the film at the place showing Jesus carrying His cross through the streets of Jerusalem. This seemed to be an appropriate time to stop and share the truth and significance of the cross.

"Jesus Christ was different from all other men," I emphasized, praying in my heart that some among that great crowd would grasp the fact of the uniqueness of Jesus.

"As you have just seen, Jesus was born of the virgin Mary through the power of the Holy Spirit." I went on to explain that His life on earth was just as perfect, as pure and as sinless as His birth had been.

"Jesus was the perfect Lamb of God," I continued. "He came down from heaven, becoming flesh like us, in order to become a necessary sacrifice for our sins, as the Lamb of God."

Then I began explaining why it was necessary that Jesus

should suffer and die on the cross. "God did indeed love Jesus, even as He loves us, but He is also a *just* God. Even though God loves us, He hates sin, and He must punish sin. Because God is righteous and just, all sinners must be punished. This is what God Himself says in His holy book, the Bible: 'All have sinned and fall short of the glory of God' (Romans 3:23).

"That is why," I said, "God was really showing us just how great His love for us is, when He allowed Christ to be crucified on the cross. Even though we are all sinners, and we deserve to be punished for our sins, God sent Jesus, the perfect Lamb of God, to pay the penalty for us.

"Jesus alone could satisfy the demands of our just God," I continued, "because He alone was pure and sinless. The tremendous penalty of the world's sin had to be paid by Jesus, and no one else. No ordinary man like you or me could pay that enormous price. Only the perfect, sinless One, the Lamb of God, could do this."

The thread of unrest continued across the audience, but nevertheless I took a few moments more to explain how God had always required, even during Old Testament times, that all the symbolic animal sacrifices had to be absolutely perfect.

"Today some people are still trying to follow these ancient ways of worship through animal sacrifices," I said in conclusion. "But this is because they do not know that the one true God has now made a way of access to Himself through Christ, His perfect sacrificial Lamb."

Some listeners at the back shouted "Blasphemy! Blasphemy!" at this, so I switched on the projector again, turning their attention back to the film.

Violence Erupts

Within moments Jesus reached Golgotha on the screen, and then the scene of the crucifixion flashed before the audience. Suddenly the unrest of the crowd boiled over, and they erupted into a wild, ranting mob.

"Blasphemers! Infidels!" came the cry, and it became a loud chant echoing across the milling crowd. Some threw stones at the projector, and others ripped down the makeshift screen. Angry shouts and insults filled the night air, and we realized that the threats of violence were moving directly toward us.

Hurriedly, we pulled our projector and the generator into

the nearest Christian home and locked the door against the angry crowd outside. We huddled together inside the house, less than a dozen Christians praying for God's protection. On our knees, we asked God to calm the enraged crowd outside, still shouting their hoarse chants: "Allah-hu-akbar! (God is great!) For shame! These blasphemers have crucified the prophet Jesus! Infidels!"

It was several hours later before the commotion outside seemed to have subsided, so that we thought it would be safe to return home. In the darkness, we quickly packed our equipment into our little blue Volkswagen, said subdued goodbyes to our Christian friends who had sheltered us, and started home on the only road out of the village to the main highway.

Muddy fields, nearly submerged by the early spring rains, surrounded us on both sides of the narrow dirt road as we drove along. Suddenly about a mile from the village my headlights flashed on two groups of men, standing on either side of the road ahead. There were about 10 or 12 men, and they were stretching a heavy rope across the road, evidently hoping to stop us.

A Spoken Word in My Ear

"Lord," I prayed fervently, "What shall I do? Show me, please show me!" I knew that there was no place to turn around, nor could I safely back up such a great distance and return to the village. And then, almost as though I heard a spoken word in my ear, I knew what to do.

I stepped on the gas, speeding as fast as possible towards the two knots of men holding the rope. As I sped by, acting just as though nothing were there, the men lost their hold on the rope and it jerked out of their hands. Still, they were able to heave heavy stones at the car before we were out of range. We drove on for several minutes before we pulled over to breathe heartfelt prayers of gratitude to God for our escape. Upon examination, we found that we had suffered no physical harm except a few dents in our V.W. and a broken back window.

It was after midnight when we reached home, where my wife was waiting for us. For several hours she had been burdened to pray earnestly for us, impressed by the Holy Spirit that some trouble had befallen us. She had even gone next door to enlist the intercessory prayers of an elderly missionary couple with whom we had close Christian fellowship. So when we drove in safely, there was much rejoicing, and together we thanked and praised God for the power of prayer which had again moved the hand of God on our behalf.

At the same time, however, as I went to bed that night, I felt very disappointed that we had not even finished the showing of the film, nor had anyone in the village been led to a saving knowledge of the Lord Jesus Christ. But obediently, as an act of my will, I reminded myself, "Success in witnessing is simply sharing Christ in the power of the Holy Spirit, and leaving the results to God," and I went to sleep.

An Apologetic Stranger

The following morning, I answered a knock at our door. A well-dressed gentleman whom I did not know stood there on the threshold. As soon as I invited him into our home, this stranger began to apologize to me for the rough treatment I had received at the film showing the night before!

"I-I hope that you are all right," he said. "I am very sorry that the people of my village became so angry with you. They cannot seem to understand that we should listen and try to understand when someone thinks differently from the way we do."

I assured him that God had kept me safe from all danger and thanked him for his concern.

He went on to introduce himself as a professor in the large university there in our city. Prof. Akram, as I will call him, had gone out the previous evening for a weekend visit with relatives and friends in the village where he had been born and reared. When he learned of the film-showing, he had joined the crowd of villagers, but when the program turned into a riot, he became greatly embarrassed by the violent turn of events against me.

I saw that my wife was preparing tea for us, so I persuaded him to be seated before I asked, "Professor, do you know why those villagers got so angry with me?"

"Of course," he sighed. "Because your film showed Jesus Christ being crucified. He was actually dying on the cross."

Insisting on the Cross

He paused a moment, then looked me squarely in the eye

and asked, "Would you please tell me something? I have searched all the morning to find you, because I wanted to apologize to you for the behavior of my village. But more than that, I want to ask you a question.

"*Why* do you Christians insist on this matter of Jesus dying on the cross? Just last night, you were risking your life out in my village, trying to convince people that Jesus really died! Surely it wouldn't take anything away from the prophet Jesus to say that God wanted to protect Him from harm — so He rescued Jesus and took Him straight up to heaven, as we believe!"

"That's a very good question," I assured him, "and I am glad that you asked me, because it's important. You see, Christianity *is* the cross! If we take away the cross of Jesus Christ, and the death of Jesus Christ on that cross, then we have nothing left!"

Prof. Akram looked mystified. "What do you mean?" he asked.

"You saw the film last night," I reminded him. "God's holy Word, the Bible, tells us that Jesus was born, and lived, and died, and rose again. The Bible even says that if Jesus did *not* die and come to life again, then our faith is worthless, and we are still in our sins, according to I Corinthians 15:12-20.

"So this is the central truth of our faith, prophesied hundreds of years before Jesus came to earth, that Jesus would die in just this way, shedding His blood as the sinless Lamb of God." I picked up my Bible and read to him Romans 5:8, "But God demonstrates His own love toward us, in that while we were yet sinners, Christ died for us."

The professor frowned in deep thought. "But it seems so cruel of God," he contended, "to let Jesus die like that. No one can think of such a tragedy, that a holy prophet from God would be killed. Why didn't God provide another sacrifice? Didn't He provide a ram for Abraham, so that he didn't have to sacrifice his son?"

"Because," I explained, "there was no other sinless sacrifice to be had! Jesus was the only perfect, holy, sinless Lamb of God, and He alone could satisfy God's requirement for a perfect sacrifice for all of our sins."

"I don't understand," he said slowly. "Why did God have to require a sacrifice for our sins? Don't you believe that God is merciful and compassionate? Of course we have all sinned, but will God not overlook our mistakes and small misdeeds, if we have done many good works and we have really tried hard to be good?"

My heart filled with compassion for this sincere gentleman who so clearly wanted to please God, and I prayed for wisdom to explain this great truth of the gospel in a simple, yet powerful, way.

Balancing Love and Justice

"Yes, God is merciful," I replied. "The Bible tells us that God has a very special kind of love for us — *agape*, which is unconditional, no matter who we are or what we have done. But that is only one aspect of God.

"God is also righteous and just, Prof. Akram," I continued, "so we must balance that with His love. That means that God is so very pure and righteous that not even the tiniest speck of sin can exist near Him. So even if we try to be very good, we could never become absolutely perfect before our holy God."

I reached for my Bible, again searching out some passages that reveal this truth. "The prophet David pointed out in the Zabur that everyone is sinful," I said, reading Psalm 14:2,3: "The Lord has looked down from heaven upon the sons of men, to see if there are any who understand, who seek after God. They have all turned aside; together they have become corrupt; there is no one who does good, not even one." I turned over to Romans 3:10-12, showing him that God had repeated these same words in the New Testament.

"God also said through the prophet Isaiah, in verse six of chapter 64, 'For all of us have become like one who is unclean, and all our righteous deeds are like a filthy garment; and all of us wither like a leaf, and our iniquities, like the wind, take us away.'"

But the verse which struck home to his heart was James 2:10 which says, "For whoever keeps the whole law and yet stumbles in one point, he has become guilty of all."

Prof. Akram looked at me in alarm. "Then there is no hope for any of us!" he exclaimed. "We are all unrighteous before God!"

"That's right," I replied, "and that is why we need the cross. The cross was God's *only* way of satisfying perfectly His own standards of both love and justice.

"You see, Prof. Akram," I said, "if God were *only* love, He could just say to us, 'Yes, you have sinned, but I forgive you.' However, God is *also* perfect justice — so He must demand a payment for our sins!"

Paying the Price

"Let me tell you an interesting story I heard about a famous judge in America," I said. "Perhaps it will help you to understand what I mean."

"It seems that this judge had a son who committed a crime. The penalty for the crime was $1,000 — but the son did not have any money to pay this fine. When the time came for the trial, the judge sat in the courtroom and heard his son proved guilty. So the judge had to read the sentence, and tell his own son that he was guilty and must pay a fine of $1,000.

"The son hung his head and admitted that he had no money to pay the penalty. Everyone wondered just what the judge would do, because he could not break the law and let his son go free. They watched in surprise as the judge came down from his bench, removed his judicial robes and came to stand by his son. Then he reached into his pocket and took out some money. He carefully counted out $1,000 and laid the amount on the courtroom bench. Then he put his arm around his son, saying, 'My son, the fine must be paid, because you broke the law. But because I am your father, and I love you, I will pay the fine!' "

The professor was nodding slowly as I concluded, "That is just what God did for us, Prof. Akram. He knew that we were guilty, and that we couldn't pay the penalty for our sins. Yet still He loved us! So He paid it Himself, with the priceless blood of the Lord Jesus Christ, the Lamb of God Who was without sin."

This illustration sank deeply into Prof. Akram's heart, and he sighed in wonder. "But why would God love us so much?" he asked after a few moments.

"That is a question I cannot answer myself," I answered with a smile. "But the fact that Jesus Christ actually died on the cross for me, to pay the penalty for my sins, proves to me forever that God loves me!"

We finished our tea together, and then I opened the Four Spiritual Laws and read through the booklet with him. We reviewed God's love, man's sinfulness, the uniqueness of Jesus Christ and the need to receive Christ as Savior and Lord. After I had read aloud the suggested prayer, I asked Prof. Akram if he would like to pray a similar prayer and invite Jesus Christ into his heart.

"I just did," he admitted. "I prayed as you were reading it."

"So now you are a Christian," I said.

Consternation flashed across his face at my words, and he responded quickly, "But you know that I cannot admit this openly! You know what would happen. I would lose my job, and perhaps even my wife and three children would be taken from me.

Secret Commitment

So for a time, Prof. Akram remained a secret believer. I met him occasionally, in a casual setting on his campus where no one could suspect that we were discussing spiritual matters. He had begun to read his Bible, and although he was afraid to take home any other Christian literature, he began to grow in his new relationship with Christ.

How significant it was that the cross became the focal point of his search. As I pondered that, I realized anew just why the cross of Jesus Christ is such a great stumbling block and offense in the Middle East.

Prof. Akram had always rejected the cross because he was blinded to its essential truth: the suffering and death of Christ on the cross is the greatest demonstration of the love of a holy God for sinful mankind. Prof. Akram, like millions of others in the Middle East, was not hardened to this truth — rather, he had never heard it!

"How tragic!" I thought to myself. "The cross is recognized around the world as the symbol of Christianity. Yet right here in the Middle East, where Jesus actually died on that cross, so very few have heard that the cross represents God's supernatural, unconditional love for us!"

I purposed in my heart to emphasize the powerful appeal of God's love among my fellow believers in the Middle East. It occurred to me that, when God actually brought into reality this dream He had given me of a large gathering of Middle Eastern Christians, perhaps several days of our sessions should be devoted to careful study on how to communicate to people God's love in a positive, clear way . . .

CHAPTER SIX

Barricades Against Belief

*". . . Always being ready to make a defense to everyone
who asks you to give an account for the hope that is in
you, yet with gentleness and reverence."*

I Peter 3:15

"What? *You* are a Christian? But . . . but . . . you come from
Pakistan! How is it that you can have such a strong faith in
Jesus Christ?"

One after another the questions come, wherever I travel
throughout the Middle East. While I have experienced many
opportunities to explain my faith in Jesus with individuals of
Muslim background in Pakistan, it seems that such openings
multiplied when I began to travel the whole region in 1973.

I am humbled repeatedly to realize the distinct advantage I
have in sharing my faith in the Middle East in contrast with my
missionary brothers and sisters from the West. The assumption remains firm — Westerners are Christians, and Middle
Easterners are Muslims. So because national Christians are
such a tiny minority in the Middle East, nearly everyone as-
sumes that I am a Muslim — and they are startled, to say the
least, whenever I begin to share the love and claims of Jesus
Christ with them.

One such man was a Turkish professor who had recently
returned from earning his Ph.D. in management in the United
States. Our meeting in Turkey was engineered by the Holy
Spirit, through the circumstances of an unusually heavy snow-
fall in the winter of 1974.

Stranded by a Delay

I was near the end of a month-long trip, and I had arrived at
the Ankara airport about 4 a.m. to catch a domestic flight to
another city. There I found that the runways were snowed in,
with all air traffic discontinued. I wasn't too alarmed at first,
until I realized that there was no way to inform the believers
expecting me in the next city that I would not make my
scheduled meeting with them that evening.

When I was finally airborne some 12 hours later, I was even more startled to realize another problem: not only would my friends not be at the airport to receive me, but I had absolutely no clue as to how to locate them, except for a post office box number! I groaned to myself, wondering *why* I had not been more thorough, at least to request some home addresses and telephone numbers from these friends! After all, I should have known always to expect the unexpected in the Middle East!

However, there was nothing I could do that Sunday night, except pray and trust God for some kind of solution. When our plane finally landed and taxied up to the air terminal, I glanced at my watch. I was supposed to be speaking to a small home gathering of Christians at just that time!

Clearing my luggage in record time, I hailed a taxi driver who affirmed with a big smile that he could speak English "a leetle." I jumped in, and then sheepishly handed him an envelope bearing the return address of a city post office box.

Amazed, the driver asked, "But where you want go?"

"That's the only address I have," I admitted, feeling helpless and rather foolish.

Fortunately, the driver was no dunce. He studied the box number, recognizing in the code the area of the particular post office. Then he slowly pronounced the name above it.

"This name," he said hesitantly, "not Turkish name. This foreign name. I know some foreigners where they live. I take you."

Shrugging his shoulders as he turned on the ignition, he said, "Maybe somebody there will know? . . ."

Needle in a Haystack

Willing to grasp at any straw, I agreed. To my surprise, in just a few minutes we pulled up near some apartment buildings built on the hillside. I hopped out of the taxi, thinking to myself, "This is like hunting for a needle in a haystack!" But what else could I do? The taxi driver was optimistic, so I should at least try.

Several apartment buildings later, it was nearing 10 p.m. and I was cold and weary. I agreed to try one more building before giving up and checking into a hotel. Inside the doorway, I peered at the dimly-lit names by the doorbell. I could hardly believe my eyes. There was my friend's name!

Eagerly I pushed the proper doorbell, but my smile faded when no response came after a good five minutes of ringing. Finally a neighbor raised her window, shouting in Turkish at the taxi driver, "They have gone on vacation!"

When he translated for me, I thought for a minute. That could hardly be the case, because this was the man who had scheduled the very meeting I was missing. However, it *was* probable that he was somewhere else tonight, attending that meeting.

I sighed in frustration. I was so close, yet I was still lost! Just as I turned to walk back to my taxi, a man walked up, looked me over carefully and asked, "Are you, by any chance, Kundan Massey?"

"I certainly am!" I admitted in relief, as this welcome stranger shook my hand and then grabbed for my suitcase.

"We're still waiting for you at our meeting," he explained, as we walked up the street to another building nearby. Never did I feel a warmer welcome than my reception in that small living room, where about 35 Turkish and expatriate believers waited for me! It was such a miracle that I had found them, so we praised the Lord together, knowing He had a special purpose in getting me there.

Introducing a Multiplication Ministry

During our time of fellowship together, I was asked to share about the work of our ministry in the Middle East and Asia. I first explained our philosophy of national leadership in each country, and then introduced the various materials and strategies which God has enabled us to develop over the years to help train and disciple Christians in the basics of spiritual multiplication.

Afterwards time was given for questions and interaction, and then because the hour was so late, we dismissed the meeting. As everyone was leaving, a lady brought her husband to meet me. He had not heard my talk, but had just arrived to take his wife home. As she introduced me to Haidar Bey, as I will call him, she mentioned that he had studied abroad and was now teaching in a Turkish university.

Assuming that he was a believer, I began to explain the sample material which I had placed on a small table for the group. "We use these two small booklets to share with people how to receive Christ, and then how to appropriate the ministry of the Holy Spirit," I said, handing him the Four Spiritual Laws and the Holy Spirit booklets.

Then I pointed out two sets of larger study booklets. "These Transferable Concepts explain the key 'how-to's' of the Christian life, starting with 'How to be Sure You are a Christian' and continuing through the ministry of the Holy Spirit in detail. Then these larger booklets, called the *Ten Basic Steps Toward Christian Maturity*, are designed for personal and group Bible study . . ."

Finally Haidar Bey's wife interrupted me gently. "Mr. Massey, why don't you explain to my husband that first booklet, about how to become a Christian?"

Looking back and forth from her husband to me, she said quietly, "Haidar Bey has a number of questions concerning our faith. Maybe you could answer them for him."

Suddenly I realized that her husband was not a believer! I turned to him, and seeing that he was eager to talk with me, I quickly offered, "I would be glad to try to answer any of your questions."

Stock Objections

Just as I expected, Haidar Bey proceeded to bring up all of the "stock objections" which Middle Easterners hold against Christianity.

"Well, first of all," Haidar Bey said, as we sat down in a corner of the room together, "it seems to me that you Christians worship three gods, not just one. Every good Muslim knows that there is only one true God!"

"Every real Christian also agrees with you that there is only one true God," I assured him. Then I explained the simple but profound truths of the trinity, stressing that it is entirely possible for God to have three different *manifestations* — as Father, Son and Holy Spirit. "After all," I said, "He is almighty God, and He can manifest Himself in any way He chooses."

I went on to explain various scriptures that present God in different forms, and Haidar Bey admitted he had not heard this before. He was even more convinced when I shared with him various illustrations of one substance having three forms — such as H_2O appearing as water, ice and steam. At length, his questions satisfied, he turned to another barricade he had erected against Christian beliefs.

Is the Bible Reliable?

"Well, anyway," he said, "I don't think that your New Testament is a reliable proof. It has been changed from the original, so that today we can't tell for sure what is the truth from God."

With friendly interest, I simply asked, "Is that right? Can you tell me who changed the Bible?

"Or when?

"Or how?

"Or *why*?"

I paused after each question, so that Haidar Bey could think about each point. Finally, he shook his head.

"Haidar Bey," I continued, "your own holy book, the Qur-'an, mentions three other sacred books which were given by God to humanity: the Tawrah (Old Testament), the Zabur (Psalms), and the Injil (Gospels). Isn't that right?"

Haidar Bey nodded, but then he frowned and objected, "Yes, but you have changed the Injil!"

"Let's consider the facts of history," I suggested. "The prophet Muhammad lived about 600 years after Christ's earthly life, didn't he?"

"That's right," Haidar Bey acknowledged.

"If you have read the Qur'an," I continued, "you know that the prophet Muhammad always speaks of the Injil as an authentic holy book, referring to it as 'God's Word.' "

Haidar Bey nodded, so I went on. "Not once in the Qur'an did the prophet Muhammad criticize the Injil and say it had been changed. So in his day, at least, it must have been pure and undefiled."

"That is very logical," Haidar Bey agreed.

With that premise established, I made a second point. "The oldest manuscripts we have today of the entire New Testament are dated 350 A.D., some 250 years before the Qur'an. In fact, there are two copies, one in London, and the other in Rome. These manuscripts are the source of the translations of the Bible being used today.

"Now," I continued, "During the 250 years between the original manuscript and these two copies, we have thousands of manuscripts which contain portions of the Injil — and if you put them all together, you can form the entire New Testament, just as we have it today.

"So it is very obvious that all of these manuscripts and quotations from the Injil had a common source — the original copy! They have never been changed, because during all these periods of history, it was the same!"

While that truth sank into Haidar Bey's mind, I added, "Besides, if God the Almighty, our Creator, wanted to send us the truth in the Injil, can you believe that He would allow the men He created to change His book into a lie?"

"No," admitted Haidar Bey. "God would protect it."

"That's right," I said. "Jesus Christ Himself said, as recorded in Luke 21:33, 'Heaven and earth will pass away, but My words will not pass away.' God protects His Word! The Qur'an itself says in Surah 10, Jonah:64, 'There is no changing the Words of Allah.' So the truth is that the Bible has not been changed at all."

Haidar Bey met my inquiring glance with understanding in his eyes, and without embarrassment he accepted this inescapable truth, saying quietly, "I believe that you are right."

One Last Question

He offered a few other objections, and I answered each simply, with love and understanding. Finally he sighed, "I see, Mr. Massey, that you have very good answers to my questions. I have never heard such logical answers before.

"But I still have one more question, and if you can really explain this to me, I will become a Christian right now!"

"What is your question?" I asked.

"I cannot understand how you can call your prophet Jesus 'the Son of God.' How can God, the one true God, have a 'Son'? You must know that this is terrible blasphemy, to think that God would have relations like that with Mary!"

Despite the smug expression on his face, as he leaned back to hear my reply, I knew in my heart that Haidar Bey was serious. He had honest questions that needed sound answers, but the Holy Spirit had made him ready to open his eyes to God's truth.

Over to one side, I was conscious that Haidar Bey's wife and another believer sat with bowed heads, interceding for this dear man as we talked. "O Lord," I prayed in my heart, "give me Your own words to speak to this man, in answer to his question and their prayers!"

"How can God have a Son?" I repeated. "Well, let's look at our reliable authority, God's holy Word.

"The Injil affirms that Mary, the mother of Jesus, was a virgin. Doesn't the Qur'an agree with that?"

"Yes," nodded Haidar Bey, "the Qur'an says that she was a virgin, and it also calls her 'blessed.' "

"And further," I said, "both the Bible and the Qur'an state that Jesus was conceived by the Holy Spirit, *not by any human agency*."

Haidar Bey nodded again.

"Well, then," I asked, "if someone is born of a virgin according to the fulfillment of prophecy, and not by any human agency but by the power of the Holy Spirit of God, whose son shall I call Him?"

The silence was long and still, as Haidar Bey thought through this concept for the first time in his life.

"It wasn't a *physical* relationship in any way at all," I said, anticipating his assumption. "It was a *spiritual* relationship."

I paused once more before saying, "In most parts of the world people go by their father's name, as a matter of identifying themselves. So it is right in this instance to call Jesus by His Father's name. Not only that, but Jesus also had the same characteristics as God the Father. Jesus gave life to the dead, stilled the storms, walked on water, knew the future, healed the sick and demonstrated many of the other supernatural qualities of God. Like Father, like Son!

"Haidar Bey," I concluded, "that's why we call Him, 'the Son of God.' "

"I see!" he cried. "I really see it now! It was not a physical relationship, as I had always thought. Of course not! It was spiritual!"

He seemed delighted over this truth, so I began to summarize our discussion by sharing with him the gospel story as contained in the Four Spiritual Laws. He pondered all this very openly, so I paused after reading the suggested prayer aloud and asked, "Would you like to pray now, and receive Christ as your personal Savior?"

Haidar Bey nodded. "But not here," he said, his eyes taking in the others in the room. "I want to be alone." I handed him the Four Spiritual Laws booklet and suggested that he go into the tiny bedroom where my suitcase had been placed.

Harvest of a Year's Prayers

When he shut the door, I turned to find Haidar Bey's wife sobbing for joy. "The believers here have been praying for Haidar Bey for more than a year now," she told me through her tears. I swallowed hard and blinked my own eyes a bit, humbled to be the one chosen to help communicate God's love and to "harvest" this man for Christ's kingdom.

Several minutes later, Haidar Bey emerged from that room and engulfed me in a warm embrace. I have never seen another man's face glow like Haidar Bey's when I asked him, "Did you ask Jesus to come into your heart?"

"Surely you can see that!" he exclaimed.

"Well, did He come in?" I persisted.

"Of course He did! He promised to come in if I asked Him, so He is in my heart right now!" he answered.

What rejoicing followed that night for all of us as we saw the first evidence that Haidar Bey had become a new creature in Christ. I could hardly go to sleep at 2 a.m., even though I had been awake for 22 hours.

Tangible Changes

The next time I came through Turkey, I rejoiced at the tangible ways in which Christ had changed Haidar Bey into a Christian husband and father. He had begun a revolutionary new life-style of honesty and integrity that amazed everyone who knew him.

But he confessed to me then that he was struggling with one great inconsistency in his life, because he could not bring himself to love or even trust the Greek people.

"Haidar Bey," I responded, "I want to share with you another very powerful concept. I want to explain how you can love others by faith." We poured over the Scriptures together that evening, reviewing these simple principles which so few Christians understand, and before I flew on I left him a copy of Dr. Bright's Transferable Concept booklet, "How to Love by Faith." On the same occasion, I was invited to share the Word of God in the service of a Greek church, so I took Haidar Bey along with me, giving him opportunity to meet born-again Greek believers who loved and followed the Lord Jesus Christ just as he did.

The next time I saw Haidar Bey, he quickly pulled me aside and confided, "I have good news. I love the Greeks now!"

He also told me something I have never forgotten.

"Kundan," he said, "do you know *why* it was that I even listened to you that first night I met you? Many other people had tried to answer my questions and to explain the gospel to me. But I never listened — because they were all Westerners!" He explained that he had never been able to shake off the impression that Christianity was somehow a western religion, but he was greatly intrigued that night to meet a Pakistani, a real "Easterner" who actively believed in Jesus Christ.

"I reasoned to myself while you were talking," he admitted. "I knew that you had lived and studied in the United States, just as I had. But you had come back and lived right in Pakistan, so I know that it was possible to live as a Christian, even in the midst of a strong Muslim environment. I knew then that it wasn't impossible for me to be a Christian, either, just because I live here in Turkey!"

As soon as I could get alone after that, I got down on my knees and thanked God for His persistent faithfulness in my life. Just to see this one man's life forever changed by the power of the living Christ was worth giving up everything that had once tempted me and tugged at my personal desires. How I praised God for bringing me back to the Middle East!

And as I thought back on this experience some years later while in Tehran, I knew that my own advantage in witnessing for Christ in the Middle East was the same powerful advantage of every other born-again believer of Middle Eastern background. That was precisely *why* the gathering I was dreaming about and praying for must focus on the training of *national* believers. I loved my brothers and sisters in Christ from the western world who were coming to the Middle East and giving themselves to be used significantly by God's Spirit; but I knew that it was the daily lives and witness of the *local* believers, filled and empowered by the Holy Spirit, with which no Muslim could argue . . .

CHAPTER SEVEN

Amid the Revolution

"So everywhere we go we talk about Christ to all who will listen." Colossians 1:28 (LB)

It was during our last months in Tehran, living through the Iranian revolution which captured the attention of the whole world from the fall of 1978 through February, 1979, that God chose to define my burden for training national Middle Eastern believers one step further, to the *lay* believer.

Less than two weeks before the Shah flew from Tehran into exile, I was returning home from a short but strategic visit with our staff teams in Lebanon, Cyprus and Jordan. The plane landed at Mehrabad Airport well after the evening curfew, so I was relieved to find that military patrols were arranging taxi passes to take all passengers to their destinations in Tehran. Three checkpoints later, I was safely home.

My wife was bursting with news of all that had happened across the city those few days I had been gone. The demonstrators on the streets were becoming more violent . . . some cars had been burned downtown . . . it was almost impossible to buy gas for the car or kerosene for heating . . . and the lines for bread and other food staples were getting longer and longer.

"But there is some good news, too!" Iqbal reported. "Some of our neighbors and others have been coming to inquire more about Jesus."

A Colonel's Cautious Search

She was especially anxious to share with me about an army colonel who lived just a few streets away from our home.

"He was disappointed that you weren't here to answer his questions," she said, "and he asked me to get word to him just as soon as you returned, so that he can come and talk with you." He appeared very eager to talk about Christianity, she observed, and was a well-educated man who seemed to be searching for the truth.

Even so, I was quite cautious when the colonel first came to see me. I let him explain that although his family was very much against the present government, he himself was committed to the Shah. As always, I kept quiet on political issues, though I wondered to myself if he could be a Savak agent, or even on the side of the new revolutionary forces. I told him that we were praying every day for the country of Iran.

But as the discussion turned to spiritual matters, I became convinced that his heart was open, receptive and even searching. He explained that during the past few months he had gone to various people among his acquaintances whom he knew to be Christians, asking them to explain Christianity to him.

Perhaps they were Christians in name only, which is common among the ethnic Christian groups across the Middle East. Many such Christians identify themselves with the symbol of the cross and follow the devout religious traditions of their families, but they have not experienced the reality of knowing Jesus Christ personally. At any rate, they had not been able to give him the clear understanding that he sought, he told me.

"I want to know the difference between my faith and Christianity," he told me on his second visit, a few days later. Then he admitted that he had watched us at a distance for some months, knowing that we were Christians. His wife and others in his family were antagonistic toward Christianity, so he had never come to speak to us, but he was surprised that a family from Pakistan would be Christians, and he wondered whether we could explain to him just what it meant to be a Christian.

Of course, I assured him that I was "more than happy" to explain the basic facts of Christianity and answer any of his questions.

A Disturbing Question

The colonel already knew some of the history of Jesus' life. So I went on to point out carefully the spiritual significance of His miraculour birth, His sinless life, His substitutionary death on the cross and His bodily resurrection from the dead. He listened with intelligent understanding, but there was still a question in his eyes.

Probing a bit, I discovered that he was disturbed over the

question of whether Christians worshiped three gods. I opened my Bible as we sat together in my office, showing him a number of Scriptures in both the Old and New Testaments that say very plainly that our God is one God.

"See what it says here in the Old Testament," I said, opening to the book of Deuteronomy. " 'To you it was shown that you might know that the Lord, He is God; there is no other besides Him' (Deuteronomy 4:35).

"And later on in Chapter 6, verse 4, we read again, 'The Lord is our God, the Lord is one!' "

Then we turned to the New Testament, where I read Ephesians 4:6, "(There is) . . . one God and Father of all who is over all and through all and in all."

"Our Bible speaks over and over again of the 'one true God,' Whom we are to worship in spirit and truth," I explained. "But people have become confused about the trinity of God, Who exists as one but manifests Himself in three ways. There is only one God, but He reveals Himself to us as God the Father, God the Son (Jesus Christ) and God the Holy Spirit."

Finite Illustrations

Frowning, the colonel raised his eyebrows and tossed up his head in the common Iranian gesture of denial. "But," he protested, "one Father plus one Son plus one Holy Spirit equals *three* — three gods! How can you believe that these three are just one?"

"Because I do not try to add them," I answered. "You can come closer to the truth by multiplying them! By that equation, one times one times one equals . . . one!"

That made sense to him, so I continued. "You are familiar with the formula of H_2O. It is only one substance, but still it appears in three different forms — steam, water and ice."

"Or take me as an example," I suggested. "I am a son to my father, a husband to my wife, and a father to my own son. Am I three people? Of course not — I am only one person, but I have three different roles or relationships."

He got my point, so I continued. "The Old Testament tells us that God appeared to Noah, Abraham and many other prophets in different ways. Sometimes God appeared in fire, other times He appeared as the 'Angel of the Lord,' or the 'still small voice.' But in each case, God's Word makes it clear that this was a manifestation of God Himself.

"These illustrations help us to understand the triune nature of God better," I concluded. "But of course we can never explain the supernatural completely through these comparisons to limited physical elements. The truth about God is deeper and greater than our finite minds can grasp."

Then we were interrupted, so he left the house deep in thought.

A Unique, Personal Savior

It was several days later when we talked again. This time our discussion went quickly to the uniqueness of Jesus Christ. The colonel was amazed as I reviewed the many unique prophecies about Jesus, made hundreds of years before and yet fulfilled precisely in His birth, life, death and resurrection.

"There has never been anyone like Jesus Christ!" he finally commented.

I took this opportunity to share with the colonel my own personal experience of coming to know Christ, years before in Pakistan.

"When I talk about receiving Christ in my heart and *becoming* a Christian," I explained, "I mean that I invited Christ to come into my life. That's just what the word 'Christian' means — Christ in one."

The colonel listened carefully as I went on to verbalize the content of the Four Spiritual Laws, explaining to him how he could experience the love and forgiveness of God through Jesus Christ. His intellectual questions on the trinity had been satisfied already, and his heart was touched by the love God had demonstrated in sending Jesus as the sinless, perfect Lamb of God to die in our place.

That day I gave him a copy of the adapted Middle East version of the Four Spiritual Laws, which we had made culturally relevant two years before for use with those of Muslim background. He still was carrying it in an inside pocket the next time I saw him.

Peace in Revolution

The last time he visited our home, I remember explaining that my faith in Christ had made me a child of God.

" 'As many as received Him, to them He gave the right to become children of God, even to those who believe in His name,' " I quoted from John 1:12.

"That's why I am not afraid," I said, "even though this revolution is going on all around us here. I am a child of God, and I am assured of eternal life with Christ, no matter what happens to my body here on earth."

I never saw him again, but after our evacuation a few weeks later, my thoughts turned to him often. Day after day the news media reported so many executions among the officers of the former Imperial Army, and I wondered about the fate of this colonel. I thanked God for leading him to my home, so that he had heard and understood the way of salvation. And I continue to pray that he has availed himself of this wonderful, free gift purchased for him by the blood of Jesus Christ.

But I also thought a long time about his admission, during one of our discussions together, that he could not seem to find out the truth about Jesus Christ from other Christians there in Iran. Reluctant to be seen talking with anyone involved in fulltime Christian ministry, like pastors or missionaries, he had sought out only laymen like himself — everyday people who seemed to face the same kind of problems that he did every week. But none of them had been able to share with him, as one friend to another, the simple truths of the gospel.

Many times I had heard the accusation hurled at foreign missionaries and even salaried national Christian workers, "Oh, they do this evangelizing and witnessing because it's their job! After all, they are paid to do this sort of thing!" But such a charge could never be made against the believing national layman who witnesses as a way of life.

That was another reason why I knew God wanted the emphasis of our large gathering of Middle Eastern believers to be on national *lay* believers, as the key to effective saturation of their own nations with the love of Jesus Christ.

Saturation Through Lay Witness

Even more than we needed Christian pastors and full-time workers in the Middle East, we needed committed lay men and women from every profession and calling in life — businessmen, teachers, government workers, homemakers, nurses, journalists, engineers, lawyers, doctors and others — who could live and witness for Jesus Christ every day in their spheres of influence. It would not be easy for them to escape from the "minority mentality" which had become a major faith barrier to the Middle Eastern believers, but once they truly understood how to give themselves to holy optimism and boldness through the empowering of God's Holy Spirit, then I was confident that our Muslim friends would begin to know who Jesus really is — the eternal Lamb of God, the Savior of the world.

I was only one man, but I personally had met and shared the love of Jesus Christ with hundreds of people in the past few years who were just like Akbar, Prof. Akram, Haidar Bey and the Iranian colonel. I had to admit that I had not found, as I shared the gospel with them, that their minds were closed, nor their hearts hardened. Very simply, they were just uninformed — they had never heard the truths of the gospel of Jesus Christ presented in a clear, inoffensive manner!

So everything continued to point toward the need of the hour in the Middle East — practical training which the national believer could apply in his daily life and witness. I knew from my own experience that this training, especially when offered in the context of a large gathering of fellow believers, would provide the necessary foundation for an unshakable commitment to the fulfillment of the Great Commission here in the Middle East. So together with my staff, I began to launch out into the greatest faith risk I had ever undertaken, a venture to be called the Middle East Leadership Fellowship . . .

CHAPTER
EIGHT

The Vision Unfolds

*". . . Lift up your eyes, and look on the fields, that they
are white for harvest."*

John 4:35

We were into the fall of 1977 by the time my vision for the
Middle East Leadership Fellowship took tangible form. The
preceding spring and summer, I had been traveling almost
steadily to various countries of the Middle East, sharing some
basic training in how to live and share the abundant Christian
life through the power of the Holy Spirit. Each time and place, I
had the happy privilege of seeing the lives of national believers transformed through these simple truths.

In each nation I visited, I interacted at length with national
Christian workers, pastors and lay believers about this persist-
ing vision from God to call together Christians from every
nation in the Middle East. Their sincere encouragement was
another confirmation, as they responded, "This is just what we
need — don't let your vision die!" The concept of a working
conference of national believers stretched their faith, and
many began to pray that they themselves could come to participate.

Simultaneously, God was allowing me to witness firsthand
a growing boldness on the part of believers across the Middle
East. National Christians and mission leaders alike were experiencing a fresh boldness of spirit to believe God for what
had always seemed utterly impossible: the task of reaching the
people of the Middle East with the loving Good News of Jesus
Christ. For decades, churches and mission groups had
cautioned, "Don't take any unnecessary risks!" or "You can't
expect normal methods of evangelism and discipleship to
work here in the Middle East." But now, God's people were
exploring realistic ways to go about the fulfillment of the Great
Commission in these difficult and needy lands.

It was dramatically clear to me that this new boldness was
matched by a growing openness on the part of people of all

backgrounds in the Middle East. In all of my years of ministry in the Middle East, never had I been more impressed by the truth of the words of Jesus, "The harvest is plentiful, but the laborers are few" (Luke 10:2). As I traveled through many countries and interacted with our staff and others, I realized that the scores of hungry hearts we encountered through our ministries were only a very tiny indication of the hundreds of thousands of Middle Easterners now ripe unto harvest — if only someone were to go out in God's timing to reap them.

First Century Believers

A highlight of my summer that year was an extended trip through North Africa, where I felt at times that I was stepping back into the company of first-century believers. My heart was touched to meet these brave followers of Jesus, all converts from Islam, who displayed such joy and courage in the face of constant pressure and persecution. I felt deeply humbled and privileged to meet with them in small groups, usually under careful cover in secret places, to share with them our basic training in how to experience the ministry of the Holy Spirit and how to share the love of Christ with others. They were especially responsive to my wife's prayer workshops and seminars, forming prayer chains and learning how to become effective intercessors for their own people.

One experience in particular showed me again how powerful all this simple training could be in the life of a national believer who was deeply committed to Jesus Christ. On the last day of our visit in one city, I saw a national brother take his Arabic Four Spiritual Laws booklet across the courtyard and begin sharing it with one of his countrymen who happened to be visiting the capital city from a faraway town. The believer had never met this young man, but he was anxious to try this new method he had just learned for sharing the love of Christ with others.

I watched with interest, because this believer was one of the most zealous I had met. He had been imprisoned many months for his faith and witness, and I had been impressed by how he had joyfully trusted God during his imprisonment for his own needs as well as those of his wife and children, who were destitute without his income.

I watched as this believer went through the Four Spiritual

Laws booklet carefully with the stranger. After some time, he closed the booklet and came back to me, reporting, "This man is very close to the kingdom!"

Puzzled, I asked, "Did you finish the booklet with him?"

"No," he admitted, "I just went through Law Three, explaining to him that Jesus Christ is the only way to God."

I encouraged him to continue through Law Four, urging him, "Please, my brother, give this man a chance to receive Jesus Christ if he is ready!"

The believer agreed and went back to explain to this man how he could respond personally to the love and uniqueness of Jesus Christ. To his utter joy, the young man was eager to pray right there with him and invite Jesus into his life.

"He told me that he only visits our city once a year," reported the believer later. "But God had prepared his heart and arranged this one time in the year for us to meet!"

Afterwards I thought about this incident and concluded, "We Christians in the Middle East have been doing a lot of sowing, but rarely do we reap any of the harvest." I had just witnessed a major clue to the problem: we had not been trained to "go on" after presenting the gospel and give people an opportunity to receive Christ.

Multiplied Confirmation

God used this experience and multiplied others like it to confirm again in my heart that the time was ripe to put my dream of a gathering of Middle Eastern believers into practical reality. So when I returned home to Tehran in September I sat down and drafted a letter to Dr. Bright. "I have had a real vision from the Lord that I would like to share with you," I began, as I related the dream that was growing in my heart. By that time the Holy Spirit had convinced me forcefully that such a large-scale gathering would be of immeasurable value in accelerating the fulfillment of the Great Commission in the Middle East by the end of 1980 and on through the coming decade.

"But the objective of this congress would not be simply to come and read papers," I cautioned. The burden of my heart was training, and I knew that only when simple, thorough training in spiritual multiplication took place would this gathering become the area-wide spiritual catalyst of dynamic proportions that God wanted it to be. My heart-cry was for real spiritual unity and loving cooperation throughout the Body of Christ in the Middle East. Therefore it was logical to begin by gathering my fellow believers together so that we could share with one another every fruitful means which the Spirit of God was using to present the love of Christ and to build strong disciples in this needy area of the world.

Dr. Bright's immediate response to my plan was enthusiastic, and by telephone a few weeks later he promised to clear his demanding schedule so that he himself could participate in this congress. I had already begun to share this vision with our national staff and the international representatives serving with Lifeagape International in the Middle East, so after Dr. Bright's initial approval we began to discuss the major details of such a gathering. There were dozens of complex considerations to which we gave much thought and prayer over the next few months.

The Perfect Location

My first concern was that such a gathering should be convened right in the Middle East somewhere, if at all possible. Not only would this save a great deal of traveling time and costs for the participants, but a Middle East location would re-emphasize the prevailing national flavor of the conference.

However, this consideration presented a number of difficulties. Nearly every location we surveyed for our conference had some significant drawback — either an unstable political situation, like Beirut, or a setting not likely to be sympathetic toward the gathering's objectives. Obviously, we wanted to maintain a very low-key image throughout the preparations and actual sessions, so it was important for security purposes that our conference site be able to guarantee closed and private sessions. This was not such a simple matter in most nations of the Middle East, where privacy and personal civil rights are often minimal.

From the first, I had considered the island of Cyprus to be one of the best possible locations for the Middle East Leadership Fellowship. Located just off the coast of Syria and Lebanon, Cyprus has strong Christian traditions dating back to the apostle Paul's first missionary journey about 45 A.D. It had become a popular conference center for the entire Middle East in recent years, offering efficient facilities, moderate prices and a mild climate. Visa formalities would be uncomplicated for most of our delegates into Cyprus, and the capital city of Nicosia would provide a relaxed, pleasant setting for our week or more of intensive sessions. So by the summer of 1978, God had confirmed in my mind that Cyprus was His choice for our conference location.

God's Timing

When I first began to put my thoughts and plans for this fellowship on paper, I envisioned an opportunity to call together my fellow believers in the Middle East by the fall of 1978. I even set some tentative dates for October of that year, falling just after Ramadan (the annual month of fasting in the Muslim world).

But I soon began to see that God was bringing together a number of circumstances to delay that schedule. For one thing, we needed several key, experienced personnel to direct and administer the complex logistics of such a gathering. For another, we would also have to go out and raise the entire budget to finance the conference, since we had no funds which could be allocated for such a project.

And then I learned of another major conference that was in the planning stages for the fall of 1978 — the North American Conference on Muslim Evangelization, which was slated for Colorado. I had been invited to participate in this myself, and our ministry did not want to compete or clash with such a key congress, even though most of the participants would be Westerners. So in light of all of these factors, it seemed wise to postpone the Middle East Leadership Fellowship for one more calendar year, until November of 1979.

Choice Personnel

Once the place and time were set, I still needed God's appointed personnel to help administrate such a gathering. Our headquarters office team was quite small, so I inquired through our international placement committee in the United States about the availability of some qualified senior staff member who could assist me as the director of our Middle East Leadership Fellowship.

Interestingly, the longer the chairman of this committee searched for such a person, the more convinced I became that he himself was the man for the job! He was filling a valuable role as the liaison between our continental directors and the U.S. staff to fill the many personnel needs overseas, but in the process, God had been putting into his heart a specific desire to invest his life and ministry in the Middle East. Just a few months after I challenged him to take this key responsibility, we learned that Dr. Bright had released him without a re-placement (an unusual exception to the policy of this minis-try!) to transfer to the Middle East.

By the time he and his family arrived in Cyprus early in 1979 to begin administrative preparations for the Middle East Leadership Fellowship, God had also provided us with an assistant and a secretary to work with him in a full-time capac-ity. How thankful I was for these skilled, trained staff members whose hearts were deeply committed to helping communicate the love of God to the people of the Middle East! They have served the Lord in an anonymous position, with a genuine servant spirit — and their 10 strategic months of involvement with the Middle East Leadership Fellowship was a labor of love that has helped to change the whole complexion of the spread of the gospel here in the Middle East. Because of their continuing, vital roles in our ministry in this part of the world, I cannot safely identify them by name. But these staff members invested themselves sacrificially to make the Middle East Leadership Fellowship (MELF) a success.

Consensus of the Believers

Once the MELF administrative team and I began to delve into the actual scope of a gathering of this nature, we realized a keen need for extensive input and interaction from a wide spectrum of national Christian believers across the Middle East. We needed to obtain the consensus of their spiritual wisdom and experiences in order to develop wise policies from the very start in many areas — defining our real objec-tives, determining what training materials to include, decid-ing which speakers to invite, agreeing on what written state-ments to make (if any), organizing how to invite participants, and evaluating what financial commitments to expect.

For that reason, we were impressed to form an Advisory Board for the Fellowship — consisting of our national staff directors and other key Christian leaders in the Middle East who could provide valuable counsel on all of these vital issues.

In order to form such a board, I first sent various staff on fact-finding trips through some key countries of the Middle East, as well as related nations of the Islamic world. Not only were they able to issue personal invitations to key individuals to serve on our Advisory Board, but they also found these trips a valuable introduction into the widely varied circumstances of the different Christian communities in the Middle East.

From Algiers to Karachi, from Khartoum to Dubai, they saw with their own eyes a cross-section of the Middle East. In some nations they were amazed to discover a vibrant, bustling evangelical church that was multiplying itself steadily, at least within the context of the ethnic Christian population. In others, they joined small handfuls of believers who met secretly in homes, singing softly for fear of detection by radical groups or secret police. This was valuable exposure for our administrative staff, and I rejoiced at the insights and vision which these experiences built into their lives as they began to shoulder the mountain of details involved in bringing this gathering into reality.

Advisory Board Consultation

Seven months before the Middle East Leadership Fellowship was to begin, we were able to bring together our 15 Advisory Board members for consultation in Cyprus. We were a diverse group of Middle Eastern believers, representing a cross-section of Christian backgrounds and ministries. Yet during those three days in April, we had a first taste of the spirit of loving unity and cooperation which was to characterize MELF itself. An outsider would have wondered to see how the Holy Spirit melted our hearts together — whether Egyptian or Palestinian, Arab, Pakistani or Westerner. We had come to seek God's direction for the months of preparation which would follow, so we began on our knees.

Together we wrestled with some hard decisions regarding the priorities we must set for such a national fellowship in the Middle East. First of all, we refined and put into writing a clear statement of the central objectives of the Fellowship. We agreed on five clear goals, each of which had to be phrased with much care to safeguard against misunderstandings or negative repercussions:

1. To motivate Christians of the Middle East to united and effective prayer. We recognize we live in a part of the world where spiritual ministry is difficult, if not impossible at times. Our work is one that must be both saturated in prayer and dependent upon divine intervention. The constant focus of the Middle East Leadership Fellowship must be on our mightiest weapon — prayer! And we must practice prayer at our sessions.

2. To hear encouraging reports of the mighty works of the Spirit of God through His church in the Middle East and around the world, motivating us to examine the task which yet lies before us.

3. To teach principles of management — both managing oneself and managing others. We will explore biblical principles that are above time and culture.

4. To make application of management principles within the church to aid church growth. We want to examine the reasons that cause the body of Christ to expand. Some are management-related, others are based upon application of Scripture, still others stem from methodology.

5. To examine effective methods of evangelism and discipleship within our culture. The presentation of the gospel must be comprehensive yet simple; cultural, yet scriptural. New believers must be taught basic Christian growth. Mature Christians must be discipled. Focus should be on the best opportunities to relate the message within our circumstances.

Comprehensive Scope

With our objectives established, we then had to consider the scope of the conference. We were not interested in gigantic numbers, but only that a significant, workable size of a congress be convened, representing the entire Middle Eastern world. We agreed upon setting a goal of 300 participants — the majority from the Middle East, but with representative invitations also going to individuals in Africa, Asia and other areas of the world with major Muslim populations.

Every one of us was committed to the premise that God desires and has directly commanded the fulfillment of the Great Commission among all the nations and peoples of the Middle East. We felt very keenly the urgency of a united, cooperative effort of evangelism, undergirded with concerned prayer, to bring about this fulfillment. So as an Advisory Board, we convenanted to pray daily that God would bring believers from every country of the Middle East to MELF. We reiterated that the entire conference was directed toward national believers, as a matter of priority, but at the same time we stressed that the presence of expatriate Christians and mission leaders ministering in the Middle East would be welcomed.

To my knowledge, this would be the first time in this century, and perhaps ever, that believers had gathered in the Middle East to consider the spread of the gospel in this part of the world. The last such conference, organized in 1906 by Samuel Zwemer in Cairo, brought together some 60 representatives — most of whom were missionaries. Our Fellowship, by contrast, would focus upon *national* Christians as a timely and historic reminder that the fulfillment of the Great Commission in the Middle East is the primary responsibility of the Middle Eastern believers themselves.

A Program to Meet Needs

We discussed the entire content and schedule of our conference, which would cover eight full days of sessions, in light of the five objectives we were committed to accomplish. There were so many topics and concepts that we were eager to include — a strong spiritual ministry from the Word of God, quality time right during the sessions for prayer, current reports of the moving of God's Spirit throughout the Middle East and other parts of the world, management training for personal and church ministries, and of course some very practical training to assist pastors and laymen in sharing their faith and building new disciples.

After we had compiled all our suggestions, I reviewed with these men a simple outline of the various training institutes which our ministry has adapted for the Middle Eastern culture. We proceeded to check off the various items on our suggestion list, and it was a thrill to discover that a comprehensive presentation of these basic workshops and seminars would fulfill all of these needs!

I cautioned the Advisory Board members that the delegates might be a bit staggered, over an eight-day period, to hear an entire Prayer Workshop, a Lay Institute for Evangelism and a Management Training Seminar. But at the same time, I explained that because my own life had been revolutionized by this training, I would recommend that nothing be omitted. The others were of one mind with me on this, even if it resulted in a more concentrated schedule than normal. That was quite a decision, when you consider how dearly we Middle Easterners love our afternoon nap!

In relation to the actual content of the Fellowship, we also drafted a list of potential speakers who would be representative of national perspectives in the Middle East, as well as outstanding leaders of the Christian world. We began to pray that in addition to Dr. Bright, many other men of God from around the world would be impressed to clear their busy schedules and even pay their own way to come and share their hearts with us.

Unique Financial Policy

Perhaps the most historic decisions we made were in regard to finances. When I first began thinking through the realities of MELF, I had estimated that a working budget of nearly $300,000 would be required to fund the conference. However, we began to pray and pare it down, and we emerged with a conservative budget of $175,000. We were able to make major cuts because of the Advisory Board's unanimous caution, "Do not pay the entire cost for participants! We do not have much 'Christian' money here in the Middle East, that is true, but God will provide — He wants to stretch our faith and show us how to trust Him for at least a portion of our costs."

So in what was a unique decision so far as Third World believers are concerned, we agreed to request every participant to trust God to provide a portion or all of his own expenses — through his own resources or his local fellowship of believers.

"What an incredible decision!" I thought to myself. And yet I knew that even though Christian resources were at a bare minimum across the Middle East, God was just as capable of providing rupees, dinars and pounds for His children as He was of supplying U.S. dollars! God was to honor that decision many times over the coming months, simply because we stepped out in total dependence upon His supernatural provision.

Cooperative Recruitment

A final consideration was our method of selecting and inviting potential participants. For reasons of security, we agreed not to publicize the Middle East Leadership Fellowship. Our invitation letter, discreetly phrased, said, "We share the mutual concern of communicating the love of God with the people in our culture." But even so, we limited ourselves to issuing these letters only by personal delivery. This posed a few problems in the more inaccessible nations, but God showed us how to follow this policy in every situation.

In particular, the Advisory Board members pledged themselves to work closely with our staff directors to recruit MELF participants. Many took the responsibility to visit neighboring countries in addition to their own. One board member sacrificed his vacation that summer to locate and recruit participants from a nearby nation closed to the gospel. Another returned home and recruited several delegates who came to MELF. But during the week before MELF, trouble flared in this man's own city and he was the only registered participant from his country who was unable to attend the Fellowship.

Others provided strategic "one-in-a-million" contacts along the Arabian Gulf, North Africa and other sensitive areas. They invested a great deal of time and money to send letters, cables and telexes to various relatives and other contacts. As a result, we were put in touch with key Christian businessmen and several Christian enterprises, as well as with some expatriate believers. Through their encouragement, a number of mission groups, Christian organizations and local churches went to considerable lengths to help us find and recruit participants all across the region.

By the time our Advisory Board meetings were concluded, it had become evident to all of us just what an adventure in faith this Middle East Leadership Fellowship was going to be! In our parting time of prayer, we knelt silently together, pen and paper in hand, asking the Holy Spirit to bring to our minds the people of His choice whom we should invite to MELF. Now and then through the stillness, I could hear pens moving and paper rustling — and I was thrilled again with the assurance that God was indeed leading us in every detail, big and small. Even then, I could not imagine all the evidences of the supernatural moving of God which still awaited us . . .

CHAPTER NINE

Characterized by the Supernatural

*"Jesus said to them, 'With men this is impossible, but
with God all things are possible.' "*

Matthew 19:26

As wonderful as it was to reflect on the great spiritual
potential of the coming Middle East Leadership Fellowship, I
found myself quite perplexed at times — and even somewhat
intimidated — over all the impossibilities that we faced in
bringing it into reality. The challenge of this Fellowship has
been the greatest "faith risk" I have ever experienced personally! But at the same time, my staff and I have thanked God
repeatedly in the months since MELF that our all-wise,
sovereign Lord persisted to "push us out on a limb" and trust
Him to bring this gathering of believers together, despite the
difficulties.

When the MELF director came to me suggesting that our
coference theme be "Characterized by the Supernatural," I
knew that this was the perfect choice for such an unprecedented gathering. How else could we pray, by faith and yet
with sound minds, that God would bring to MELF our prayer
target of 300 participants from 30 countries? Just weeks before
the Fellowship, we still did not have a single contact in several
of the more difficult countries, let alone any way to get visas
and go in to locate potential delegates! And how could we plan
with human ingenuity to print all the necessary materials in
the required languages, and somehow get them past unsym-
pathetic "official eyes" to our conference? Where were we to
find qualified Christian interpreters to man the instantaneous
translation booths in four or five languages for eight strenuous
days? The questions kept popping up, and very few of them
had any answers, so we agreed unanimously that MELF would
have to be "Characterized by the Supernatural" from start to
finish to ever happen!

Some weeks later God gave us the right verse to further
emphasize this concept of complete dependence on Him to

move in miraculous ways. It was the strong, unswerving promise of Jesus in Matthew 19:26 which I had chosen back in 1977 as my special verse for that year: "Jesus said to them, 'With men this is impossible, but with God all things are possible.' " Many times in the last weeks before MELF I turned to that passage in my Bible, reminding myself and our staff that God wanted us to stand firm on His promise. Together with our Middle East headquarters staff team in Cyprus and our various staff teams in countries across the Middle East, I had committed myself to the Middle East Leadership Fellowship — so we could only take Jesus at His words, expecting Him to do many miracles of the impossible to bring it about.

10,000 Praying Christians

As summer approached, we were impressed to begin praying that God would raise up at least 10,000 Christians around the world to pray daily for this Fellowship. In particular, we knew how important that would be during the month of November, as the actual conference was underway. Just voicing that request to the Lord took some faith, because we could not even publicize the fact that such a conference was going to be held!

Undaunted, my staff sent out very carefully worded prayer requests, writing to their friends and supporters to explain, "Please pray for the Middle East Leadership Fellowship. This one week in November could help change the whole course of history in the Middle East." God also gave us wisdom to prepare a very discreet brochure and an explanatory letter that could be used on a limited basis with Christian individuals, churches and other groups in Europe and the United States.

For many weeks we prayed that God would somehow use these efforts to mobilize at least 10,000 believers around the world to become our "MELF Prayer Warriors," interceding daily for this small but unique Fellowship. We did not suppose that we would ever know whether we had even come close to our goal, but still we were convinced that this prayer target was from God.

To our surprise, we learned several weeks after the MELF sessions were over that every October donor to the Campus Crusade for Christ ministry in the United States had received an urgent request on that month's gift receipt to pray that the

Middle East Leadership Fellowship in Cyprus during November would "dramatically accelerate evangelism in the Middle East." In other words, at least 105,000 tithing, concerned Christians had been alerted to pray for this Fellowship! What an incredible answer this was to our prayers. We had also printed several thousand prayer calendars for the month of November, mailing them to western Christians interested in the Middle East so that they could pray in specific terms every day of that month for MELF.

Our MELF administrative team and the Lifeagape office staff truly set the pace in prayer themselves those months prior to MELF. First we set aside an additional half-hour every day for united prayer in regard to all of our MELF needs and problems. Then we reserved an extended noon hour each week for prayer and fasting, with the first day of each month given entirely for the same purpose. To all of us, prayer had become the highest priority — the very same priority which we wanted it to have during the Fellowship sessions! A number of times, after discussing a long list of our current "dilemmas" with the MELF director, I was so encouraged by his conclusion: "Kundan, we need to discuss this with the *real* Director of MELF. Let's pray!" So we did, pausing many times throughout each day — and each time we saw God dissolve all of the puzzling details and transform them into blessings.

Some of our answers to prayer still cannot be shared in print, but one classic example involved the dilemma of flying our 42 Egyptian delegates to Cyprus. When we first checked air flight arrangements for this important delegation, we learned that the only feasible air flight from Cairo into Cyprus' Larnaca Airport required an overnight stop in Beirut. But visas for war-torn Lebanon were difficult to get, and each visa required an official certificate from the Egyptian government, stating the specific purpose of each passenger's trip. The last thing we wanted to do was to draw attention to the fact that so many Egyptian Christians were flying together to this Fellowship! So we were hesitant to confirm the large block of seats through Beirut, even though we knew of no other alternative.

By late October, we knew why God had kept us praying for His solution. Our travel agent called to report that both Cyprus Air and Egypt Air had just negotiated to alternate direct flights four days each week from Cairo to Larnaca — beginning

November 1st! And if that was not enough to rejoice about, we also learned that this direct flight saved approximately $100 on each passenger's ticket. This was a total saving of more than $4,000 of the Lord's money!

God's Economy

Another major answer to prayer was the financing of this whole conference. Even though budgeted funds were not available, we determined to trust God to provide the entire budget before our Fellowship actually began. We were not required to pay for all the air fares, hotel bills and material shipments in advance — but, of course, during the week of MELF everything would fall due, in cash and in full! As a staff family, we prayed with one mind and spirit that the entire $175,000 would be received on or before November 12th, the opening night of the Fellowship.

During the summer, I took nearly six weeks to help raise finances in the United States for MELF among key Christian leaders and businessmen who were keenly interested in the spread of the gospel in the Middle East and around the world. But despite a very warm reception and many significant investments, the months flew by, and we entered October with only $58,000 — far short of the $175,000 we needed.

I remember glancing over the long list of those donors, touched to see that hundreds of individuals had given, some far beyond their means, to this Fellowship for the cause of Christ in the Middle East. A number of our own staff members gave very sacrificially, to the extent of helping to subsidize entire national delegations. But regardless of the love those gifts represented, we still had only a third of the cash we knew that we must have in hand within six weeks!

At that point, we could only assume that the Lord wanted us to rest upon His faithfulness to somehow provide the lacking funds. So we continued on, in faith, acting just like we had the rest of the money in the bank! The weekend before MELF was scheduled to begin, our financial picture had still not changed substantially. In fact, it was not until the day the delegates began arriving at Larnaca Airport that I learned through Dr. Bright that God had just provided three large cash gifts in the United States that were earmarked for the Middle East Leadership Fellowship. One of those substantial checks was signed by a young man only 22 years old! So there was great joy and thanksgiving in my heart, as I stood before the opening banquet of MELF to deliver the keynote address, to realize that God had miraculously provided for the entire financial need of this unique Fellowship!

With the Ink Still Drying

Materials were needed in five languages at MELF, requiring orders from all corners of the Middle East as well as from the United States and Europe. In some cases, our dedicated staff in various countries met an array of "impossible" deadlines in order to edit, proof and print the necessary materials— management manuals, prayer guides, and other tools for evangelism and discipleship which had been developed and adapted for the Middle Eastern cultures. In others, they asked that we all pray daily that God would somehow blind the airport customs officials in their countries as they attempted to bring out these precious materials in their luggage on their way to the Fellowship. Scores of supernatural events took place in answer to all of these prayers as the materials were safely routed to Cyprus.

To the unnerving of our administrative staff in Cyprus, not a single shipment of the MELF materials, many ordered months in advance, arrived in Cyprus until 10 days before MELF was scheduled to begin! In fact, the bulk of the Arabic, Farsi, Urdu, French and English materials cleared customs during the first four days of the MELF sessions. One of the last sets of Arabic materials was hand-delivered from our Lebanese printer, who had to send his son from Beirut along with the shipment. This young man, formerly a sniper with the militia in Beirut, invited Christ into his life with the staff member who met him at Larnaca Airport!

On the final day of MELF, there was still one outstanding shipment of Arabic materials to be cleared out of airport customs. It contained vital materials that every Arab delegate needed to carry back home in his personal luggage. Tables were set up for literature distribution after the appropriate session, but the minutes ticked on by and still we did not have the materials. Finally, just 15 minutes before the session concluded, one of our staff members arrived at the hotel from the airport with the cleared shipment. We sighed happily, reminded that God's timing is never late.

Qualified New Hands

When the pace of MELF preparations accelerated in the last two months before the Fellowship began, we saw God provide another desperate need: additional administrative staff. We marveled that He had not only provided five more individuals with willing hands and hearts — but He also gave us senior staff members whose unique administrative qualifications matched perfectly with our particular organizational needs at MELF. We kept this project team at a steady run during those demanding weeks, but they were faithful to walk in the power of the Holy Spirit, and as a result they also saw many supernatural answers to prayer.

For example, the secretaries poured much concentrated prayer over a certain Nashua photocopy machine rented for the two weeks surrounding MELF. Due to the security required for our Fellowship, it was necessary to wait until the weekend before the sessions began to print and assemble the entire conference manual. In addition, countless handouts and inserts were printed and distributed throughout the week to delegates, along with daily schedules and announcements. To complicate the process, everything had to be typed twice, in both Arabic and English!

For an average of 16 hours a day for two straight weeks, our secretaries manned the photocopy machine, recording more than 60,000 copies. And yet the machine only broke down once. When that happened, God brought an Egyptian delegate up to the fourth floor of the hotel to ask a question at the MELF office. Seeing their mechanical difficulty, he volunteered, "I know just the man to help you!" He disappeared down to the sessions and returned in a few minutes with another Egyptian — a man who "happened" to sell and service Nashua photocopy machines for a living! The man quickly tore the machine apart and repaired it, restoring it to perfect working order within minutes.

So many other miracles occurred that they cannot be numbered. My wife had prayed in particular that we would have pleasant weather, so we all rejoiced when the Lord gave us unusually lovely, clear skies throughout those two weeks. The next week the rains came, beginning one of the hardest winters Cyprus has had in years.

In a conference of that size, we had anticipated some medical needs, and God had provided a Christian American doctor who worked in the Gulf area as our consulting physician. By God's grace, however, his services were not required for any major medical problem.

The Cypriot government had provided a very fine and discreet team of security police to give our sessions round-the-clock protection, and they handled every minor occurrence with exceptional tact.

All of the last-minute schedule changes seemed to improve the sessions rather than hamper them. Such was the case with the need to arrange a larger room for the ladies' luncheon featuring Vonette Bright on Friday — since 25 more guests made reservations at the last minute!

So it was only appropriate, after all of the multiplied answers to prayer that we had experienced, that our staff gathered for a very special thanksgiving celebration that November (the American Thanksgiving Day fell on the day after MELF concluded). What an occasion that was for all of us, weary but overjoyed, as we made a gigantic listing of God's supernatural answers to prayer throughout the months of preparation as well as during the Fellowship itself. "We can never pray too much!" I thought to myself that day, realizing that the Middle East Leadership Fellowship had concluded just as it had begun — with a day focused on prayer, the greatest privilege and power available to the Christians of the Middle East.

CHAPTER TEN

Born and Bathed in Prayer

*"If My people who are called by My name humble them-
selves and pray, and seek My face and turn from their
wicked ways, then I will hear from heaven, will forgive
their sin, and will heal their land."*

II Chronicles 7:14

"Prayer shall be our first priority at the Middle East Leadership Fellowship," our Advisory Board had declared. So it was
only appropriate that we open our sessions with a special day
set aside for prayer and fasting. We were committed not only to
talk about prayer but also to practice it — united, specific,
believing, fervent prayer.

Significantly, our opening address that first morning came
from a dear brother in the Lord whose life and ministry of
prayer is a great blessing around the world. Sergio Garcia
Romo, the director of Latin American affairs for Campus
Crusade, flew around the world from Mexico City to challenge
us on "Prayer Characterized by the Supernatural." His entire
message struck home, because five times every day those of us
living in the Middle East see a very visible form of prayer. Each
time, the minaret's resounding call to prayer causes the devout
to go to their knees, even on the busy streets. Such a respectful,
faithful emphasis on prayer in everyday life constantly reminds us that people everywhere truly seek personal communication with God.

In his introduction, Mr. Garcia made clear the ultimate
purpose and motivation of our prayer lives. "We are a
privileged generation," he began. "Never before has there
been such a potential for fulfilling the Great Commission in the
entire world. God has given us a special opportunity to see that
happen in our generation, but whether it does or not depends
upon us. We cannot appropriate the power which God intends
us to have to carry out His plan unless our lives are lived on the
basis of His principles.

"We need to realize that the Christian life is a battle, and prayer is one of the areas that is most often on the front lines of attack. I have found in my own ministry that encouraging a spirit of prayer is a constant and continuing battle, demanding faith, perseverance and work."

Then he proceeded to outline some basic conditions or principles which God's Word requires if our prayers are to be characterized by the supernatural:

1. *We need to know God.* "You, as a Middle Eastern Christian, are a reflection of your own concept of God," Mr. Garcia said. Therefore, he stressed that all of the wonderful, divine attributes and character of God need to fill our minds throughout the day.

2. *We need to seek God.* Quoting that beloved call to prayer and repentance, II Chronicles 7:14, Mr. Garcia reminded us, "People who are in love often give each other close-up pictures of themselves. God loves us, and so He has given us a close-up picture of Himself in the person of our Lord Jesus Christ. Prayer is the main way to get to know God, in combination with His Word."

3. *We need to exercise faith and obedience.* "Faith is the basis of our prayers, the foundation," Mr. Garcia said. "Faith includes anticipation of that which cannot be seen . . . an understanding or discernment into the ways of God . . . a fundamental decision to obey God . . . an action to bring things from the spiritual world into the physical world."

Mr. Garcia explained that it is not proper to say, "I am very poor in my prayer life." Instead, we should say, "I am very poor in my perception of God, and therefore I do not pray and seek His face." Again he stressed that we must saturate our minds with the attributes of God and the truths of His Word as an act of our will, because we become what we think.

4. *We need to make supernatural plans.* "We should make plans so big that unless God is in them, they are doomed to failure!" Mr. Garcia exclaimed. "I know that the Middle East seems so difficult for the gospel to penetrate," he continued, "but it is part of the Great Commission of Jesus, Who told us, 'You shall be My witnesses . . . even to the remotest part of the earth' " (Acts 1:8). He urged us to pray and plan toward the salvation of whole cities, tribes, nations, continents and cultures.

In summary, Mr. Garcia once more reminded us, "Praying

supernaturally is basically knowing and seeking out the object of our faith — our Almighty, Supreme God. It is praying according to the Scriptures, in line with God's will, based not upon our own resources or strength, but upon the character and thoughts of God. Then we have the right to expect supernatural results — even more than we had ever thought, according to Ephesians 3:20!"

"Who is God to you?" he asked in conclusion. "No Christian is greater than his conception of God."

The Dynamics of Prayer

My wife and I were particularly delighted to have Mrs. Bright come to Cyprus to lead a joint demonstration of the five-hour Prayer Workshop for our Fellowship. Not only does Mrs. Bright generate much love and respect wherever she goes, but we have found her gracious enthusiasm to be contagious as she shares how to release the power of God in the world today through believing prayer. Mrs. Bright opened the introductory sessions of the Prayer Workshop by outlining the basic principles of prayer in the life of the Spirit-filled Christian.

First my wife, Iqbal, shared the importance of prayer. "Basically," she explained, "prayer is communicating with God. A the key to releasing God's power, it is love in action, the breath of our spiritual life. And yet, the average Christian prays less than five minutes a day! Why? Because most Christians either do not know how to pray, or they lack motivation due to boredom or discouragement." She challenged us to join the early disciples in their plea, "Lord, teach us to pray!" After this Mrs. Bright shared the meaning of prayer and how to pray.

Who can pray? Mrs. Bright quoted freely from the Scriptures as she stated that those can pray who belong to Christ, who pray in the name of Christ, who have clean hearts, who have a forgiving spirit and who come in faith.

Why pray? Again Mrs. Bright brought out clear reasons from God's Word: we pray to glorify God, to obey His command, to have fellowship with God, to follow Christ's example, to bring results and to foster spiritual unity.

To Whom do we pray? "Our prayer is directed to the Father, in the name of the Lord Jesus Christ, through the Holy Spirit," Mrs. Bright summarized.

JESUS LEUR DIT...

MAIS TOUT EST POSSIBLE A DIEU »   MATTHIEU 19:26

WITH GOD ALL THINGS ARE POSSIBLE   MATT 19:26

A day of prayer, fasting and repentance marked the opening of the Middle East Leadership Fellowship.

Vonette Bright speaks on intercessory prayer.

The distinctive MELF Prayer Booth

Iqbal Massey introduces the
Dynamics of Prayer Workshop.

Dr. Bill Bright
teaches on the power
of praising prayer.

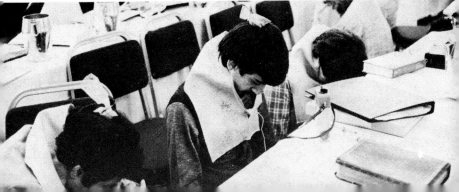

When should we pray? The Bible stresses that we are to pray constantly throughout each day, as well as during a special time set apart daily and in regular group meetings with other believers.

What should be included in prayer? Mrs. Bright shared the simple formula of ACTS, so that we could remember easily the four basic components of prayer: Adoration, Confession, Thanksgiving and Supplication.

How can we pray with confidence? Encouraging us to picture a great vault up in heaven, Mrs. Bright explained that abiding in Christ was like the combination lock to those mighty resources of God made available to us through prayer. Three other necessary elements for praying with confidence are asking, believing and receiving.

Practical Methods

Then Mrs. Bright brought these basic principles down to a very personal level. Very briefly, she explained two methods or types of prayer that have revitalized her own prayer life in recent years — conversational prayer and praying through the Scriptures. *Conversational prayer* is particularly helpful to encourage shy or new believers to pray aloud in a group. Participants in this method of prayer limit themselves to a very few words or sentences, speaking to God directly in a spontaneous manner as if He were indeed right there in the group with them. In this way, various individuals contribute to the "conversation" until one topic is finished, and then move on to another. The delegates broke into small groups of four to six individuals to practice this very refreshing approach to group prayer, and I could hear the soft murmurs of prayers all across the conference room for several minutes.

Then the method of *praying through the Scriptures* was introduced. My wife suggested that we turn to some of the Psalms or certain chapters of the New Testament as a basis for small-group prayer. After reading each consecutive verse from the passage, we were then to "pray back" these words and thoughts to God, again keeping our prayers short, in everyday language. What a delightful time of praise and worship this was for all of us! Some groups prayed in Arabic, others in Urdu, Persian, French or English — but in each case we were praying according to the will and Word of God Himself.

Hindrances to Prayer

My wife then reminded us of God's requirement that we pray with a clean heart, according to Psalm 66:18: "If I regard wickedness in my heart, the Lord will not hear." She listed some of those sins which can so easily short-circuit our relationship with God and thus prevent the answers to our prayers — selfishness and wrong motives, lack of compassion, lack of domestic harmony with one's mate, children or parents, pride, disobedience, lack of faith, an unforgiving spirit, failure to pray according to God's will, failure to know God's Word and abide in Christ, hypocrisy, wrong attitudes (such as impure thoughts, jealousy, worry, guilt, discouragement, critical spirit, frustration, aimlessness, etc.), lukewarmness and loss of first love for Christ. Silently before God, we confessed any such sin which the Holy Spirit brought to our minds, claiming God's promise to us, "If we confess our sins, He is faithful and righteous to forgive us our sins and to cleanse us from all unrighteousness" (I John 1:9).

The Family Prayer Habit

Following a mid-day break, when most of the delegates who were fasting went to their rooms to be alone with God, an afternoon section of the workshop was devoted to the importance and value of family prayer. "The Christian family is definitely a minority in the Middle East," my wife emphasized, "so our only spiritual feeding as believers comes either from the church or from within the home. Our homes should be the primary source of spiritual education. From their earliest years, our children must be taught how to pray and how to understand and apply God's Word, the Bible." After suggesting ways of beginning the "family prayer habit," she also discussed at length how to help accelerate prayer in the local church, in order to support the pastor and church members, as well as to initiate a growing outreach into the community.

Intercessory prayer, as a subject in itself, was addressed in detail by Mrs. Bright. "The greatest privilege granted to man is access to the very throne of God," she reminded us. "Today Jesus Christ is interceding before the Father for us, praying that the world will believe in Him and in God's love for them through our lives. Thus, we can have complete confidence that

God hears and answers every request we make which coincides with this great purpose of our Savior.

"We can define intercession," Mrs. Bright explained, "as a special form of prayer asking God to do something on behalf of some other person, or a nation or circumstance. It is not the same thing as praying for ourselves, because when we intercede we stand between God and another to plead their cause." She related how in many instances intercession had changed the course of history — Moses stood in the breach between God and His people, pleading with God not to destroy them (Exodus 32), and in Ezekiel's day God again looked for one of His servants who would stand in the gap for a sinful nation (Ezekiel 22:30). "God *wants* us to intercede with Him to deliver people and nations from destruction," she emphasized.

Intercession for Officials

In particular, Mrs. Bright stressed the priority of our responsibility to pray for world rulers and all those in positions of authority. "Whether they are good or bad, we should intercede for them," Mrs. Bright declared. "Those who are good need God's guidance and help and protection. Those who are bad need to hear about His love for them and His gift of new life through the Lord Jesus Christ. Men in public office everywhere carry great responsibilities and exert far-reaching influence. Their decisions affect your church, your city and your nation. Even corrupt officials can be influenced by our prayers! So we should exercise the power we possess to intercede for them before God's throne.

"Finally," Mrs. Bright concluded, "we are to live a life that prays. It isn't the words we use, but the life we live that prays. We may have the most organized plans and prayer techniques, we may keep the most beautiful prayer diaries — but all this will avail us nothing unless our life is in proper relationship with God. The Lord will not motivate, direct or fill an unclean vessel. On the other hand, He will respond mightily to the prayers of a righteous person, according to James 5:16, and history proves that even a small remnant of cleansed, committed believers can move the hand of God to bring about amazing results."

It was a simple summary of truth with which she closed, and yet it was a profound thought for all of us: "An extraordinary working of God in the Middle East today is going to require extraordinary people — and extraordinary people will only result from extraordinary lives of prayer. So upon *you* rests the key to a supernatural, extraordinary moving of God's Spirit in the Middle East — the powerful weapon of intercessory prayer!"

The delegates closed their looseleaf notebooks, now having in their hands detailed notes that would enable them to present the same Prayer Workshop content themselves once they returned home. They also had as reference material a special "Mini Prayer Diary" printed for the Middle East in Arabic and English, a resource booklet filled with pages of practical helps to enrich the believer's personal prayer life.

The Prayer Solution

As a powerful conclusion to the Prayer Workshop, Dr. Bright came to the platform to speak on "Prayer: The Solution to a World in Crisis." As full as our minds and hearts were at that point in the late afternoon, the message which he was to share from his heart and the response which followed were to set an unusual tone to the remainder of the Fellowship.

"It is my conviction," Dr. Bright began, "that God's Word teaches us that God judges, chastens or blesses a nation because of the believers in that nation. In other words, the children of God can bring blessings upon their nation if they meet God's conditions, but if they disobey, then God will chasten their nation." He went on to remind us of the examples of Jonah, who ran away from fulfilling God's commission — thus bringing a storm endangering everyone who was on board the ship with him — and Achan, whose greed and disobedience brought defeat upon his people the next time they went into battle. "But once Achan's sin was judged and punished, then the blessing of God came upon his nation again!"

Then Dr. Bright brought home the analogy to us in the Middle East. "The reason why the Middle East is not being evangelized is not because of the hardness of Muslim hearts — it is because of the cold, unbelieving hearts of the Christians! However, if real revival ever comes to the Christians in any Middle Eastern land, regardless of how tiny a minority they are, then I assure you that the Muslims around them will say in amazement, 'Oh, if I could only know this God who gives such blessing and peace and joy and excitement and wonder to those who follow Jesus of Nazareth!' "

Continuing, he said, "I am convinced that we will only see the Middle East reached for Christ when Christians here begin to believe God and obey Him. There may be only a handful of Christians in your entire country, a fraction of one percent — hardly visible or measurable. But when the Spirit of God comes upon the believers, the supernatural will take over, and a miracle will begin to take place.

"You of all the people in the world know that I do not exaggerate when I speak of the urgency of the hour here in the Middle East, and everywhere else. Today the whole world is aflame, and the tides of atheism run strongly against us. But some time ago, while I was thinking about the great threat of overwhelming trouble to come, God spoke to me in an unusual way. As I reflected on the chaos of wars and invasions occurring everywhere, it was as though God said, 'This is My doing. I am the One responsible for making godless nations afraid of one another and at war with each other — just as I caused the armies of Ammon and Moab and Mt. Seir to destroy each other many centuries ago, when they had united to march against Judah.' "

The Spirit of Jehoshaphat

Dr. Bright went on to review for us the account in II Chronicles 20 where King Jehoshaphat's immediate response to the news of the coming attack of his enemies was to call his people to fast and pray. God instructed this righteous king to organize a choir to march out in front of those three formidable armies, singing praises to God! When they did so, God caused the armies of Ammon, Moab and Mt. Seir to destroy each other.

"God spoke to me through that passage," Dr. Bright said. "It was as if He promised, 'If My people around the world will come to me in the spirit of King Jehoshaphat, and humble themselves and pray, and seek My face, then I will do for them what I did for King Jehoshaphat.' "

He shared with us how some months ago, he had been impressed to call together some of the Christian leaders of America, asking them to join in the spirit of Jehoshaphat to pray that God would have mercy on the United States, to allow the Christians of that country to help get the gospel to the world while there is still time. "I love my country, just as you love yours," he stated, "but I am chiefly interested in seeing the fulfillment of the Great Commission throughout the world in these next few vital months and the years that may follow."

Then he shared with us a recent impression which God had laid upon his heart and that of his wife as they meditated over II Chronicles 7:14: "If My people who are called by My name will humble themselves and pray, and seek My face and turn from their wicked ways, then I will hear from heaven, will forgive their sin, and will heal their land."

"What does it mean to seek God's face?" he questioned. "I think that it means to see God as Isaiah did, in all of His purity and holiness and righteousness. As a result, Isaiah immediately realized his own sin and unworthiness. When we seek God's face, we are able to see our own unworthiness and humble ourselves, and pray and turn from our wicked ways.

A Symbolic Expression

"Recently Vonette and I have been impressed by God that it is proper for Christians to do something tangible as a symbolic, outward expression of the inward desire of our hearts to humble ourselves before God. This is to follow the example of those like Mordecai, Esther, Daniel, Jeremiah and others who put on sackcloth and ashes to symbolize abject penitence."

After reviewing this practice as observed throughout the Word of God, Dr. Bright invited all of us to join him in a symbolic demonstration of sincere repentance and supplication to God on behalf of ourselves and our nations. He cautioned us that it was not the wearing of a symbolic strip of sackcloth or a small packet of ashes that would please God. "Rather, it is what goes on in our hearts," he explained. "It is the spirit within us that God will honor."

Along with the other Fellowship delegates, I fell to my knees that afternoon, shedding tears of confession and compassion as never before in my life. I asked God to humble and cleanse me, so that He could work without hindrance in my life and throughout His church in the Middle East in a supernatural way. This moving demonstration of repentance set the tone for a holy humility and spirit of dependence upon God among us all throughout the remainder of the Fellowship.

One national staff member commented, "I think that we all
got to our feet after that experience with a new sense of personal responsibility before God to be holy people, reaching
our own countries and all of the Middle East for Christ."
Another individual, a participating layman, exclaimed. "This
day has been a new call to prayer for the Middle East. I will
never forget this experience for the rest of my life!"

As we rose from our knees, Dr. Bright concluded, "My
friends, the Middle East will not be reached by great preaching. It will not be reached by the miracle of the media. God is
the One Who touches the hearts of men, and He will do this
when His children obey Him! It is then, and only then, that
God will begin to act."

The Power of Praise

It was late in the evening when the delegates came together
again for a closing message on "The Power of Praising God in
Prayer" from Dr. Bright. This was the same concept which had
so liberated me during my first year of ministry in Pakistan,
when Dr. Bright himself had demonstrated its truth and power
by example. So even though we were all weary after a long day,
my heart was eager with anticipation as Dr. Bright shared
these wonderful truths.

"Prayer in itself is a supernatural activity," Dr. Bright reminded us, "but within the framework of prayer there is
special supernatural power in praise to God." He then reviewed 16 of the many reasons listed in God's Word to explain
why praise is so important in the life of every Christian:

1. Because God alone is worthy of praise.
2. Praise helps us to glorify God, which is our major
   objective in life.
3. Praise draws us closer to God.
4. Praise liberates us from negative thoughts, attitudes,
   motives and action.
5. Praise is contagious.
6. Praise helps us to seek first the Kingdon of God and
   discover God's will for our lives.
7. Praise breaks the power of Satan.
8. Praise is a witness to carnal Christians and non-
   Christians.
9. Praise makes us more sensitive to hear God's voice.

10. Praise helps us grow in faith.
11. Praise leads to greater obedience.
12. Praise prepares us for heaven.
13. Praise helps us to be more grateful to God.
14. Praise makes for a more joyful life.
15. Praise enhances human relationships.
16. Praise is a supernatural expression of faith.

Momentum of Prayer

The following seven days of the Middle East Leadership Fellowship were enveloped in this great spirit of praising prayer. Every morning the participants streamed over to the side tables, to sign their names on the large colored Prayer Wheels which had been on display at the opening registration line. Delegates were able to participate in the constant cycle of 24-hour chains of prayer every day by signing their names on 15-minute segments during the day and half-hour slots through the night hours as "Night Watchmen."

To encourage this momentum of prayer, a unique Prayer Booth was erected in the far corner of our conference room. Constructed of signcloth in the shape of two praying hands, the little edifice was painted by Costas Averkiou, a famous Cypriot artist living in Nicosia. The booth was just large enough for one person to sit or kneel, and contained a small stand with a card file of prayer requests and Bibles in Arabic, Urdu and English. Even during the messages and training sessions, this Prayer Booth provided a private place to pray, and most of the time the tentflaps were closed — sometimes with the occupant's shoes placed carefully outside the entrance, according to the ancient Middle Eastern tradition of respect and reverence.

When God's Holy Spirit moved in such supernatural ways during the MELF sessions and in the months to follow, I knew that it was only because of this prevailing emphasis on prayer which took practical precedence over every other activity at our Fellowship. Again and again, my thoughts went back to that wonderful promise which has become God's "telephone number" for me, Jeremiah 33:3 (KJV): "Call unto Me, and I will answer thee, and show thee great and mighty things which thou knowest not."

CHAPTER
ELEVEN

The Supernatural Life-style

*"I have been crucified with Christ; and it is no longer I
who live, but Christ lives in me; and the life which I
now live in the flesh I live by faith in the Son of God,
who loved me, and delivered Himself up for me."*

Galatians 2:20

As Dr. Bright stood before more than 200 participants at the Middle East Leadership Fellowship to begin his series of messages on the ministry of the Holy Spirit in the life of the believer, my mind went back to the last time he had visited the Middle East, in the spring of 1977. He had shared those very same messages in four different nations, and in each instance hundreds of Christians had come to say, "I have read God's Word for years, but I have never understood these truths about the Holy Spirit until now! Thank you for making it so simple and practical for me."

One of the most dramatic experiences my wife and I had shared on that trip with Dr. Bright and his wife, Vonette, was a miraculous train ride through Pakistan. At that time a revolution was brewing to unseat Prime Minister Bhutto from power in Pakistan, and the news every day was filled with reports of severe political unrest.

I was hesitant to take Dr. and Mrs. Bright into such a potentially explosive situation, even though our staff across Pakistan were launching during their visit the "New Life in Christ" movement of cooperative evangelism and discipleship among all the churches and Christian organizations in that nation. When I discussed this decision with Dr. Bright, I could only marvel at his reply: "Kundan, if someone offered me a million dollars to go to Pakistan right now, wouldn't I go? Yet the souls of men and women all over Pakistan are worth much more than this, so we *must* go."

By faith, we boarded our flight and landed safely in the Lahore airport, arriving just in time to rush Dr. Bright to a combined Sunday morning worship service of all the churches

90

in the city. It was very hot and humid, and the large church was bursting with people. God began a great work that day. For five days, Dr. Bright explained the great truths of the Holy Spirit simply, through an interpreter, and the lives of many hundreds of believers were revolutionized.

On the closing day of our sessions in Lahore, the disturbances and bloodshed which had come to a lull across Pakistan during that week revived again as the Opposition Party demonstrated against the government. The riots caused all domestic and international flights to be cancelled, but miraculously we were able to reserve train seats to Karachi, where our next meetings were scheduled. At the conclusion of Dr. Bright's challenge on the Great Commission, we rushed to the railway station, knowing that a nationwide "wheel" strike had been called the following day to halt all trains, buses and cars.

Mobbed at the Railway Station

As we arrived at the railway station, we saw a huge mob of people, somewhere between 5,000 and 10,000 demonstrators, rushing toward us in an angry wave, intent on burning the train and the station. We ran quickly into a large waiting room and locked the door, not knowing what would happen. As the crowds outside began shouting and breaking up everything they could find, Dr. Bright prayed, thanking the Lord for the situation! Just as he finished, the federal security forces moved in with helmets and machine guns and dispersed the mob.

We saw no other alternative before us but to board the very train which these demonstrators had vowed to burn en route to Karachi, and so later that night we began a 24-hour journey on the train. What an experience that was! At one station, the other passengers became hysterical with fear over reports that the Opposition Party would attack the train, but our small party decided to praise the Lord, and we started singing! We knew that the train just ahead of us had killed 11 people who were lying on the tracks to try to force it to stop, and that an enraged mob had in retaliation burned that train. But we knew that we could trust God — and as we entered the station, we saw military troops protecting both sides of the track with cocked guns.

I suppose that nothing was more solid proof to me that Dr. Bright "practices what he preaches" about trusting God and walking in the power of the Holy Spirit by faith than the supernatural calmness he displayed on that train ride. All of the Christians in our party believed that God was going to protect us somehow, but only Dr. Bright possessed such positive confidence that he got into his pajamas and peacefully slept through the night! The rest of us stayed awake and dressed, somehow hesitant to relax and trust God.

When we arrived in Karachi, the imposition of martial law and a strict curfew order prevented us from conducting the planned meetings, but still Dr. Bright met with key Christian leaders of the city in his hotel room, and God impressed us all with the urgency of launching a Here's Life thrust like "New Life in Christ" in Karachi as soon as possible.

With a sigh, I brought my thoughts back from that harrowing but blessed experience in Pakistan to our conference room in Nicosia, where Dr. Bright had begun to speak. No matter how many times I had heard this great truth, it was profitable to dwell again on how to appropriate the power of the Holy Spirit in everyday Christian living.

The Most Important Discovery

"Learning how to be filled with the Holy Spirit is the most important discovery any Christian can make," Dr. Bright was saying. "Tragically, multitudes of Christians do not know how to be filled with the Holy Spirit Who is Himself God, the third Person of the trinity, co-equal with God the Father and God the Son. But this condition is so important that Jesus told His disciples not even to begin their ministry until they had been filled with the Holy Spirit, as it says in Acts 1:4,8.

"What exactly does this mean?" Dr. Bright questioned. "What can it mean to each one of us?" With powerful simplicity, he answered, "To be filled with the Spirit simply means to be filled with Christ, and to be abiding in Him.

"When that is true," he continued, "we will automatically produce spiritual fruit of two sorts. First, Christ, Who came to seek and to save the lost, will, through the power of the Holy Spirit, produce through us the fruit of souls won to the Lord, according to John 15:16 and Matthew 4:19. At the same time, the fruit of the Spirit (love, joy, peace, patience, gentleness, goodness, faithfulness, meekness and self-control) will become increasingly evident in our lives.

"Both of these results relate closely to another great blessing that comes automatically when Christ becomes all in all to us and we are filled with His Spirit: the Word of God becomes illumined and meaningful to us as the Holy Spirit applies it to our lives. All three of these results grow together to bless us with all spiritual blessings in heavenly places in Christ (Ephesians 1:3). Believers who have discovered this wonderful truth of the Spirit-filled life are victorious Christians, living the abundant life that Christ came to give us.

"But if such an adventurous, exciting, victorious way of life truly is available to every believer," Dr. Bright asked, "then why does the average Christian continue to live in defeat, enduring a miserable, up-and-down kind of life? There seem to be two reasons for this sad state. First, most Christians *lack knowledge* of just how much God really loves them and how great is His power which He makes available to them. They do not understand their spiritual birthright that belongs to them from the moment that they receive Christ.

Living Like Paupers

"Second, the average Christian is not filled with the Holy Spirit because of *unbelief*. He is afraid of God, and he does not trust Him — perhaps he fears that God will require something impossible of him, or take away all his pleasures. He is like a poor sheep rancher I heard about in Texas, a man named Mr. Yates. Mr. Yates was so destitute that he was living on a government subsidy and feared he would lose his last possession, an unproductive sheep ranch. Then some men asked permission to drill a wildcat oil well on his land, and they struck a huge, untapped oil reserve that made Mr. Yates a millionaire overnight! Mr. Yates had owned that oil all the time, but because he did not appropriate it, he was living like a pauper."

Dr. Bright smiled as he looked out over the participants and said, "You may be asking yourself right now, 'How can I strike oil like that, and be filled with the Holy Spirit?' There are a few simple facts to grasp concerning this. First of all, you became a Christian by faith, and at that moment Christ came into your life through the agency of the Holy Spirit. Therefore, you do not have to beg God for what is already yours. You are to walk in the Spirit by faith, and faith alone, although several factors contribute to your heart preparation: the desire to live a life that will please the Lord, the willingness to surrender the control of your life to Christ according to God's command in Romans 12:1,2 and the confession and cleansing of any known sin that the Holy Spirit calls to your attention.

"There are two very important words to remember in regard to being filled with the Holy Spirit," Dr. Bright continued. "The first is *command*. God commands us in Ephesians 5:18 to be filled with the Spirit. The other word is *promise*. God promises that He will always answer us when we pray according to His will. So we can pray in confidence, believing that He will fill us with His Spirit — not because we deserve to be filled, but on the basis of His command and promise."

Then Dr. Bright clarified an important point. "It is not by prayer that we are filled, however; it is by faith. Nor is being filled with the Holy Spirit a once-and-for-all experience. It is a continuing process, like breathing. As we learn how to be filled with the Holy Spirit all the time, as a way of life, we begin to experience the reality of walking in the Spirit by faith."

As he concluded, Dr. Bright gave all the MELF participants an opportunity, with bowed heads, to pray a simple prayer of faith, asking God the Holy Spirit to fill and control their lives. A number stood to their feet afterwards to acknowledge that for the first time in their lives they knew on the authority of God's Word that they were filled with the Spirit.

A Supernatural Life

In his following message, Dr. Bright addressed himself to the practical "how to's" of walking in the Spirit. "The true Christian life is a full, abundant, purposeful and meaningful life," he began, "and though it is not complex or difficult, there is a paradox to it. It is so simple that many stumble over its simplicity, yet it is so difficult that only Christ Himself can live it. It is a supernatural life, only achieved as we walk in the Spirit and thus allow the Lord Jesus Christ to live His abundant life within us in all His resurrection power!

"This does not mean that we will not have problems," he went on, "but it does mean, however, that we can freely cast all of these problems on the Lord. The secret of success in all this is to practice what I call *spiritual breathing*. This is such a powerful truth that if I only had one message to share with the entire Christian world, it would be how to breathe spiritually.

Dr. Bill Bright spoke daily at MELF sessions on the ministry of the Holy Spirit in the life of the Middle Eastern believer.

MELF participants ponder the truths of the Spirit.

It is just as essential to our spiritual lives as physical breathing is to our physical lives.

"The first step is to *exhale*, or breathe out. You must first agree with God that your sin or sins, which should be named to God specifically, are wrong and are therefore grievous to God. Then, you acknowledge that God has already forgiven you through Christ's death on the cross for your sins. Third, you repent, which means that you change your attitude toward your sin, forsaking it and giving it up, so that the Holy Spirit can enable you to change your conduct. Instead of doing what your old sinful self wants to do, you can now do what God wants you to do.

"After that," Dr. Bright explained, "you go on to the second step, which is to *inhale*, or breathe in. You appropriate the fullness of God's Spirit by faith, knowing that it is God's command and therefore His will for you to be filled with the Spirit, and that it is His promise to grant your request when you pray according to His will.

"We need to practice spiritual breathing continually," Dr. Bright emphasized, "because we dare not allow sins to accumulate in our lives. We need to exhale them as soon as we recognize them, turning from them completely in the power of the Holy Spirit. I urge you to keep 'short accounts' with God. Our path is not easy, and there are many temptations and difficulties along the way. But even though we expect to face many a spiritual conflict, we as believers are living a supernatural life — Christ lives in us!

Attacking Forces

"The conflicts will stem from three different forces that attack us: the world, the flesh and the devil. According to the paraphrase in the Living Bible, the world and its desires involve 'the craze for sex, the ambition to buy everything that appeals to you, and the pride that comes from wealth and importance.' The flesh in biblical language means simply the old sin nature which is part of our innate self-will and pride. The devil, or Satan, is a real foe who prowls around like a hungry lion, looking for some victim to tear apart. He is indeed formidable, but God's Word assures us, 'Greater is He (Christ) who is in you than he (Satan) who is in the world' (I John 4:4b). So God's spiritual armor can protect us from all three of these enemies."

An important clarification was made at that point by Dr. Bright. "We should note that temptation is not sin," he explained. "Temptation is the initial impression to do something contrary to God's will. Temptations come to all men, even as they did to our Lord, but they are not sin in themselves. They become sin only when we continue to think about them, allowing a desire to develop into lust, which in turn leads to the actual act of disobedience. We can only resolve such a major conflict when we surrender ourselves, by an act of our will, to the control of the Holy Spirit. Then we can face our temptations in the power of Christ, not our own strength."

Another major point which Dr. Bright developed was the necessity for each one of us to know our rights as a child of God. "It is impossible to experience our resources in Christ without spending time with the Lord, who is the source of our strength," he declared. Drawing upon God's Word, he reminded us that Jesus Christ, in all of His resurrection power, actually lives within us, making available His great strength and enabling us to be the fruitful witnesses He commands us to be.

"As believers, we are to live by faith, not by feelings," he stressed in his closing point. "Valid feelings are the by-product of faith and obedience," he explained, "but to seek after feelings repudiates God's command to live by faith. For Christians, the object of our faith is God and His Word. God's Word says that all things work together for good if we love God, so on the basis of this promise we can logically follow His command in I Thessalonians 5:18 to give thanks in all things. To do this, regardless of the situation, is to demonstrate our faith in God, and this pleases Him."

I had heard Dr. Bright make a similar statement many dozens of times, but still I thrilled once again when he said, "One of the greatest privileges of my life is to trust God, learning how to walk by faith. What a great opportunity is ours to walk with the King of kings every day of our lives, from the time that we awaken in the morning until we go to bed at night.

"Every morning my first thoughts as I awaken are of Christ, with the prayer on my lips, 'Oh, Lord, I thank You that I belong to You, that You live within me, and that You have forgiven my sins and made me Your child. Now, as I begin this day, I thank

You that You will walk around in my body, love with my heart, speak with my lips and think with my mind. By faith I acknowledge Your greatness, Your power, Your authority in my life, and I invite You to do anything You wish in and through me today.' Oh, what an adventure awaits those who trust in the Lord, who walk in the fullness of His power!"

Anger Can Be Exhaled

That evening as the MELF delegates quietly left the conference hall to return to their rooms for the night, I caught thoughtful expressions of understanding on so many faces. I was reminded of that same expression dawning on the face of one Arab brother several years before, when I had shared that same message with his small Bible study group. Afterwards he stood and confessed, "A few days ago I had a big fight with my wife, and I became very angry." He glanced over at his wife across the room, and then continued. "I shouted that she was spending too much money, and if that was the way she was going to act, I was just going to burn this whole roll of bills that I pulled out of my pocket!"

He sheepishly explained that he went to his store and there burned part of one bill, along with a lot of paper that he cut to the same size! "Then I stormed back home and showed my family all the ashes, insisting, 'See, if you waste all of my money, then I will just burn it!' My wife told me the next morning that she knew I had just burned paper, not the real money, but I wouldn't admit it, and I stayed very angry with her and my children."

The Arab believer turned to me in front of the whole group and declared, "Now I understand what I should do as a Christian. I have just confessed my anger to God, and here before all of you I am asking my wife to forgive me. Now please excuse me, because I am going straight home to wake up my five children, and ask them to forgive me, too!"

What a beautiful example that was in my memory of the principle of spiritual breathing, and how the Holy Spirit can use this practice to cleanse us from everything that displeases God. I rejoiced in those thoughtful expressions on the faces of the various Fellowship participants, because I knew that they had discovered, even as I had many years ago, the key principle to walking in the Spirit.

A New Way of Life

The following evening, Dr. Bright was scheduled to share one of my favorite of his messages on the Spirit-filled life, "How to Witness in the Spirit." As he introduced his subject, he related that statistics in the United States show that it takes more than 1,000 laymen and six pastors to introduce one person to Christ in a year! Subconsciously I added the thought, "And it's probably even more than that here in the Middle East."

I recalled the time we began training key pastors and laymen in preparation for a major evangelistic thrust in Lahore, Pakistan, almost two years before. Most of them had known Christ and been involved in Christian work for many years, but one after another they came and confessed to me and our staff, "This is the first time I have ever introduced anyone to Christ."

After we had shared with them this message on "How to Witness in the Spirit," a group of them went out for a special day of witnessing on the streets of Lahore. One very influential Christian layman exclaimed, "Oh, I have wasted the last 30 years of my life! I have never gone out and openly talked to people about Jesus, because I didn't think that anyone would listen, and some might even become angry. But now I see that people are eager to learn about Jesus!"

Again I was reminded of the fact Dr. Bright was just sharing before our Fellowship sessions, "There are two basic reasons why the majority of Christians have never introduced anyone to Christ. The average Christian is not living a victorious, vital, Spirit-controlled life, and the average believer does not know how to communicate his faith in Christ effectively to others. Bible study and prayer are essential to your spiritual growth," he stressed, "but they are no substitute for witnessing!"

Formula for Fruitful Witness

He went on to discuss a spiritual formula from God's Word of eight ingredients that he asserted "will transform your life and witness and cause you to be fruitful for God in a way you have never experienced before. Now some of you may be skeptical, but let me call to your attention the fifth chapter of Luke, where our Lord is speaking to a great multitude on the shores of Lake Galilee. After Jesus had finished speaking from Simon Peter's empty boat, He said to Simon, 'Put out into the deep water and let down your nets for a catch.' Simon explained that they had fished all night and caught nothing, but in obedience he let down the nets . . . and they filled with so many fish that the nets began to tear! Peter and the other fishermen with him were so overwhelmed at this that they left their nets and followed Christ.

"I promise you," Dr. Bright declared, "that if you follow this simple formula to share Christ, it will enable you to be regularly and consistently fruitful. Many of you, like the early disciples, will find this to be the most exciting and rewarding experience that this life has to offer, and you will leave the nets of your present business and professional involvements to follow Christ in the great adventure of fishing for the souls of men in your nation and around the world."

Be sure that you are a Christian, began the formula. "It is not enough to be a good, moral, religious person, or even to be a church member," explained Dr. Bright. "We must receive Christ into our lives by faith, believing that when we invite Him to come into our hearts, He will come in, just as He promised in Revelation 3:20. It is not our invitation that saves us, but rather it is our faith. If you are not sure today that Christ is in your life, I invite you to ask Him right now to come into your life. Then thank Him that He has come in, just as He promised to do, and never insult Him by asking Him repeatedly to come in."

I marveled again in my heart as Dr. Bright slowly offered a suggested prayer for the delegates to pray after him to receive Christ:

"Lord Jesus, I need You. Thank You for dying on the cross for my sins. I confess and repent of my sins, and I open the door of my life and receive You as my Savior and Lord. Thank You for forgiving my sins. Take control of the throne of my life. Make me the kind of person You want me to be. Amen."

I knew, on the basis of hundreds of similar experiences, that there were several people in the room who, in the privacy of their hearts, were for the first time sealing this personal assurance of their eternal relationship with God through Jesus Christ. And I was thankful for the repeated example of Dr. Bright never, never to assume that "everyone is a Christian here today," and pass by a chance for someone to receive Christ and find assurance of salvation.

Second, *be sure that there is no unconfessed sin in your life.* "Christ's death on the cross has paid the penalty for our sins — past, present and future," Dr. Bright reminded us. "However, when we confess our sins, agreeing with God concerning them, Christ's death on the cross becomes meaningful to us. There is nothing we can do to add to Christ's sacrifice, but confession of our sins is necessary and scriptural, according to I John 2:1-6. We must practice spiritual breathing as often as necessary."

Third, *be sure that you are filled with the Holy Spirit.* "Just as we received Christ into our hearts by faith," explained Dr. Bright, "so we understand by faith that we are filled with the Holy Spirit. Being filled with the Holy Spirit is a matter of faith, not feelings, although valid emotions result when we live by faith and obey God."

Fourth, *be prepared to share your faith in Christ.* "Through a few hours of intensive training this week, you will learn one effective way to communicate to others your faith in Christ," Dr. Bright promised. "As you learn a simple presentation of the Four Spiritual Laws which has been culturally adapted for fruitful use here in the Middle East, keep this principle in mind: It is our responsibility to abide in Christ and follow Him; it is His responsibility to make us fishers of men."

Fifth, *pray.* "We have been talking about prayer and praying all this week, but we cannot emphasize it too much," Dr. Bright said. "God is not willing that any should perish, so as we are filled with the Spirit, and witnessing in His power, we must continually ask God to draw men to Christ and cause other believers to grow spiritually as they serve the Lord. The scriptural order is to talk first to God about men, and then talk to men about God."

Sixth, *go.* "Do not wait for men to come to you," Dr. Bright cautioned, "because Jesus Christ has already commanded us to go and tell the good news to all men. Arrange your personal priorities so that you are sharing Christ regularly with others. Do not be discouraged if some refuse to receive Christ. Success in witnessing is simply sharing Christ in the power of the Holy Spirit and leaving the results to God."

Seventh, *talk about Jesus.* "Avoid arguments," Dr. Bright

counseled us, "and do not be sidetracked with peripheral matters such as talking about the church. Simply share Christ in love as Paul wrote to the Colossians, 'So everywhere we go we talk about Christ to all who will listen, warning them and teaching them as well as we know how. We want to be able to present each one to God, perfect because of what Christ has done for each of them' (Colossians 1:28, LB)."

Eighth, *expect results.* Dr. Bright stated, "One of the greatest lies of the century is that men do not want God. The fact is that men are hungry for God — they need only to be properly approached."

An Impossible Assignment

As he concluded his remarks on this point, my eye caught the glance of a participant from North Africa. I studied him for a time, recalling the time I had shared this same message a year before in Algeria. Everyone knew that it was impossible for the believers there to go out and take the initiative to share the gospel with others, but nevertheless the Spirit of God impressed me to assign them to do just that!

An hour later, we were riding a city bus with an Arab staff member and some of the national believers. I was sitting at the back with my wife when I began to hear one voice raised above the murmur of voices on the bus. It was our Arab staff member who was sharing the gospel with the bus conductor, reading loudly from the Four Spiritual Laws booklet. The entire bus quieted down as people listened curiously. After we got off at our bus stop, a well-dressed, obviously educated passenger waited for a moment and then approached the staff member.

"I have never heard such things as this before!" he exclaimed. "Can you give me this little book, so that I can learn more about this Jesus?" Our staff member was overjoyed to talk with him for some time, and the national believers were highly encouraged by this example of witnessing as a way of life. The next day, every one of the 40 believers participating in our training had shared the gospel with at least one other person!

Yes, the people of the Middle East are hungry to know God in a personal way — and how thankful I was for this Middle East Leadership Fellowship that was helping equip us all to better communicate the love of Christ to everyone around us.

CHAPTER
TWELVE

Bridges to the Unknown

*"God our Savior . . . desires all men to be saved and to
come to the knowledge of the truth."*

I Timothy 2:3,4

As the seminars on evangelism and discipleship got underway on the second day of the Middle East Leadership Fellowship, I wondered how many of the participants were thinking the same thoughts that I had voiced many years ago to Dr. Bill Bright: "This presentation of the Four Spiritual Laws just will not work in my country!"

When Dr. Bright had pursued the subject with me, I had admitted, "Yes, I do use the Four Spiritual Laws here in the United States, and they are effective. But I won't even get past Law One in Pakistan!" Nevertheless, in response to Dr. Bright's prayers, faith and encouragement, I agreed to try it.

The response was phenomenal to me. Never would I have dreamed that across Pakistan, men and women, students and laymen — from all levels of society and all religious backgrounds — would respond to the gospel when they heard it presented in this reasonable, simple manner. I knew that one reason my witness was fruitful was the fact that I was witnessing under the power and control of the Holy Spirit, not in my own strength and wisdom. But I also knew that the Four Spiritual Laws is the most effective tool I have ever found for the communication of the truth about Jesus Christ among my own people. Rather than being the "American device" I had first thought it to be, the Four Spiritual Laws is an international method of sharing the gospel — adhering both scripturally and culturally to the needs of the Middle Eastern peoples.

So as the first MELF training seminars began, scattered in small sections in various rooms of the hotel, my heart was praying continually that my fellow believers would listen with open ears and hearts to the various national and continental directors leading their seminars. Each delegate in that first session would begin by memorizing the same simple state-

103

ment I had learned years before, "Success in witnessing is simply sharing Christ in the power of the Holy Spirit and leaving the results to God."

Before reviewing the strong benefits of the Four Spiritual Laws, the seminar leaders explained at the outset that this is only one of a number of methods to share God's plan of salvation to others. "However, it is one very fruitful method," they said, "so we would suggest that you try this 'transferable technique' in your personal witness and ministry."

In each seminar the leader first demonstrated the actual use of the Four Spiritual Laws with another individual, and then grouped the participants in pairs to practice reading through the booklet with each other. In every session that followed, the same sequence was used — demonstrate a live situation, and then allow the seminar participants to practice it with each other. In that manner the delegates learned various ways to introduce the Four Spiritual Laws to an individual, how to give opportunity to receive Christ, how to give assurance of salvation to those who respond, how to handle common questions individuals often ask, etc.

Mutual Research Sessions

In addition to this basic training which was shared, I was impressed that we needed to include some sessions dealing directly with the unique approaches to follow in sharing the gospel and building disciples here in the Middle East. It was certainly vital that all of our delegates, representing as they did a wide spectrum of nationalities and backgrounds from all over the Middle East, be able to pool their experiences and viewpoints through mutual research and consultation.

We therefore devoted six hours of our schedule to practical research sessions, delving into such topics as "The Local Church's Involvement in Evangelism and Discipleship," "Methods of Cooperative Evangelism," "Socio-political Culture in the Middle East and the Message of Christ," "Use of Mass Media in Middle East Ministries," and "The Gospel and Contemporary Islam." We were privileged to have leading national Christians moderate these discussions and later deliver cumulative reports of their findings before the entire Fellowship. I regret that the nature of these significant sessions does not permit their reports to be published at this point.

This was also an ideal opportunity to share the major framework and guidelines which our ministry has developed through the past 20 years in the Middle East. By way of introduction, six major principles for fruitful witness were emphasized:

1. "God so loved the people of the Middle East, that He gave His only begotten Son . . ." Because God's motive for man's salvation comes out of His pure, unconditional love, we must also love each and every individual around us. Only through this unconditional love will the gospel truly be communicated to our Middle Eastern neighbors.

2. We do not need to know fully the religion and the religious book of another in order to share the love of Jesus with him. However, we do need to know our own message well. Of course, our knowledge of another person's religion will help us to build a bridge between what he believes and what the Bible teaches, so we should learn this well (See Appendix I).

3. We do not argue with him, since that will put him on the defensive. Instead, we explain in a friendly manner, "I am sharing what *I believe* is the truth. It is up to you to decide."

4. We never criticize his beliefs, his book or his prophet, confident that when we show him Christ revealed in all His glory, he will be drawn to Him, the Sun of righteousness, like iron to a magnet.

5. We do not try to prove various doctrines of the Bible to him before he believes that the Bible is the Word of God. Once he accepts the Bible as God's Word, then he also has to accept whatever it teaches, even the difficult parts. The Bible becomes his final authority in matters of faith and conduct, as it is for us. So we draw our teaching on the virgin birth, the trinity, and the resurrection of Christ from the Bible itself, rather than trying to read into it these teachings.

6. We avoid talking to him about Jesus Christ in the presence of his friends or any group of people. His religion requires him to reject any other religion, so only when he is alone with an individual will he feel free to share his views and listen to the Christian point of view.

Background of Islam

We presented the following outline on the background of Islam as the minimum knowledge any believer should acquire in order to help him build bridges toward effective witness:

A. *Articles of faith*
  1. Belief in one God (Allah).
  2. Belief in God's angels.
  3. Belief in God's prophets, including Jesus Christ, Moses and Muhammad. All are equally respected, especially Jesus.
  4. Belief in God's Scriptures: the Torah (Pentateuch), the Zabur (Psalms), the Injil (New Testament) and the Qur'an. All four are considered to be equal messages from God to man, but all except the Qur'an are believed to have been changed — thus necessitating God's giving of the Qur'an. However, every Muslim is asked also to believe and obey the holy books revealed by God's messengers.
  5. Belief in the "last day," or Judgment Day, and fate.
  6. Belief in salvation attained through works and faith (in the Pillars of Faith), although the ultimate decision is in God's hands.

B. *Pillars of Islam*
  1. Recitation of the creed, "There is no God but Allah, and Muhammad is His prophet" (Ash-Shahadah).
  2. Prayer (As-Salat), a ritual performance five times a day.
  3. Alms (Az-Zaqat) given to the needy.
  4. Fasting (As-Saum) for one month during Ramadan, from sunrise to sunset every day.
  5. Pilgrimage (Al-Hajj) to the Holy City of Mecca.

Basic Agreements

The following beliefs among the Islamic peoples should always be kept in mind as *basic agreements with the Christian faith:*

A. God is One, the Creator of heaven and earth.
B. All men have sinned.
C. Jesus Christ:
  1. Was born of the virgin Mary (clearly stated in the Qur'an).
  2. Was the Word of God, "Logos" (Kalimat-Allah).
  3. Was conceived by the Holy Spirit without sin in the womb of Mary, and lived a sinless life.

4. Performed miracles, raised the dead, opened the eyes of the blind and the ears of the deaf.
5. Is close to God, and will intercede for men in the last day.
6. Was to be born, die and rise again to life (Surah 19, *Maryam*, Mary: 33; Surah 3, *Al-i-'Imran*, The Family of Imran: 55).
7. Is coming back again.

D. God sent the Torah, Zabur and the Injil as His inspired Word.
E. God redeemed the son of Abraham by providing a sacrificial lamb (Al-Adha).

Basic Disagreements

In contrast, we recognize the *basic disagreements* of Islamic doctrine with the Christian faith:

A. The concept of the Son of God is rejected. The Qur'an says: "He is Allah, the One! Allah, the eternally Besought of all! He begetteth not nor was begotten. And there is none comparable unto Him" (Surah 112, *At-Tauhid*, The Unity: 1-4).
B. Another common teaching is that Christ was not crucified. The belief is that God blinded the Jews, so that instead they crucified someone whom God had made to look like Jesus. The common belief is that it was either Judas Iscariot or Simon of Cyrene (who carried Jesus' cross) who was crucified as the substitute.
C. The concept of the trinity is rejected, because it reminds them of paganism. They believe Christians worship three gods, which is considered the blasphemy of "Shirk" or polytheism, which means to put someone in partnership or company with God. By popular belief, the Christian trinity is thought to include God, Jesus and Mary, rather than the Holy Spirit as the third Person.
D. The common belief is that the Old Testament and the New Testament, although given by God without error, were later changed by men and thus now are no longer reliable as God's Word to man. According to the Qur'an, if we still had the original texts, then they could be studied. Muslims believe that it was because of this corruption of God's Word that God gave the Qur'an to Muhammad.

E. In Islam, salvation comes through both works and faith, with special stress placed upon works. One must believe all of the Articles of Faith and perform all of the Pillars of Islam whenever possible. On the Day of Judgment, a scale will weigh one's good works against his bad works to determine whether his destiny is heaven or hell.

(See Appendix I for a more complete discussion of these five doctrines.)

Explanation was also given that there are four basic types of people in the Middle East with whom the Christian believers will share the love of Jesus Christ:

1. The *nominal* person. This individual goes to prayers, and reads from the Qur'an sometimes, but he has relatively low involvement otherwise. Some laymen and students are detached to the extent that they are even agnostic.

2. The *fanatic*. This individual is highly involved and very outspoken in support of his faith, although typically he does not have much formal education — either religious or secular.

3. The *educated, involved* person. This individual is schooled and devout in his faith.

4. The person *with one Christian parent*. This individual, because he has one parent (usually the mother) who comes from Christian background, will usually have more knowledge of Jesus Christ from a Christian standpoint.

The majority of Middle Easterners fall into the first category, as nominal Muslims. They do not know much about their own religion or about the religions of others. Their knowledge about Christ is limited to what they may have heard from the Qur'an and to what exposure they may have had to Christians or Christian literature. This exposure may be either positive or negative, and will vary from country to country and from individual to individual — depending upon the percentage of Christians in their country, the reality of the spiritual life of those Christians, and the freedom the Christians have to share their faith.

Therefore, it is important at the outset to find out how much any given individual knows through previous exposure. The best way to do this is to begin sharing the gospel message with him. Since some spiritual facts are common to both faiths, they will serve as bridges from the known to the unknown.

The Authenticity of the Injil

One of the most practical adaptations of training given in these specialized sessions of MELF was sample dialogue presented for explaining the authenticity of the Injil (Gospels) to a Middle Easterner. Often when we share the gospel from the Four Spiritual Laws with an individual, the person responds, "No, I do not want to receive Christ, because I do not believe that Christ was ever crucified." Because he is convinced that the New Testament we have is changed, we must prove to him that this could not have happened. Then, as a devout Muslim, he must believe every word in it. Through this dialogue, the New Testament will regain its authority, becoming to him the Word of God. This is an essential step for him to accept the teachings on the crucifixion, the trinity, the virgin birth and other concepts vital to Christian doctrine.

This is a sample pattern of a conversation to establish the authenticity of the Injil, with "C" representing "Christian" and "N" representing "Non-Christian." This presentation was developed by one of our Arab directors who has ministered effectively among Muslims for a number of years.

C - Do you want to receive Christ now as your personal Savior and Master?

N - No.

C - Why?

N - Because I do not believe Christ was crucified.

C - Why do you think He was not crucified?

N - Because the Qur'an says so.

C - But the Injil says that He was crucified, died and rose from the dead. This is very clear in several chapters of the Injil.

N - The Injil you have is changed.

C - Can you prove that it was changed? (Pause) Who changed it? (Pause after each question.) What parts were changed? Why was it changed? When was it changed? Where was it changed? Where is the true copy?

N - I do not know. I cannot.

C - If God the Almighty, the Creator, took all the trouble to send us the truth in the Injil, is it reasonable that He would allow created man to change His book into a lie?

N - No.

C - If God sent the Injil to guide man, what should He do with His Word?

N - He should protect it.

C - If man changed the Word of God, who would be stronger — man or God?

N - Man. But this is impossible! God is Almighty!

C - If God did not protect His book, the Injil, how can we be sure that He protected the other books, and that man did not change them, too?

N - That is right!

C - The Qur'an tells the believer to study the Injil, and contrary to popular opinion, *nowhere does the Qur'an say that the Injil was changed.* This means that up to the year 600 A.D. the Injil was not changed. The original manuscripts from which our present translation of the Injil is taken date back at least 300 years before the Qur'an. Let me share with you a simple diagram that shows why I believe that the Injil was not changed.

(Draw the following diagram)

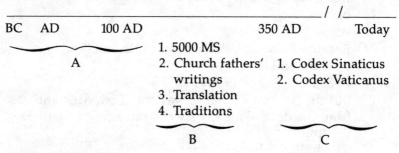

(Explain as follows:)

The original writings of the Injil were written in the first century (Period A in the diagram).

The oldest manuscript of the whole Injil is dated 350 A.D. So more than 250 years before the Qur'an, this Injil was in circulation. This copy was found in the monastery of St. Catherine in Sinai. For that reason it is called *Codex Sinaticus.* It is displayed in the British Museum in London, where you can see it for yourself, if you go there. A sister copy exists in the Vatican Library in Rome. It is called *Codex Vaticanus.* It came to us from the same time, 350 A.D. We have used mainly these copies to translate our Bible that we have today. So we will call this period, between 350 A.D. and the present, Period C in our diagram.

Let us call the period between A and C the period B. It covers the period of 250 years from 100 A.D. to 350 A.D. It is a bridge between A and C. Period B has thousands of manuscripts of portions of the Injil from many parts of the Roman world. They all agree among themselves.

We have also the writings of the church fathers who were scattered throughout the Roman world. They wrote books full of quotations from the Injil. All of their quotations agree among themselves, even though they wrote in different times and places. If we collect all these quotations we can form the whole Injil we have today except for some five verses. These verses are greetings or salutations and do not affect the basic, important teachings of the Injil.

Now, if in period B the manuscripts and the quotations from the church fathers all agree among themselves, it means that they have *one* source. That source should be A, the original copy. This means that A = B.

If we compare B with C, we find that they are the same, which means that B = C. Now, if A = B because B has one source, and if B = C by comparison of the two, then A = C by substitutions.

Consequently, the Injil was never changed. It was the same during all periods of history. God protected His book in a marvelous way. If it is the Word of God, then we have to obey it.

Do you believe that the Injil is authentic?

N - Yes. (He might be hesitant and want to think this over until a later time. In that case, make an appointment with him, and at your next meeting continue.)

C - Do you believe that Christ died in your place?

N - Yes.

C - Do you want to receive Him as Savior and Master?

N - Yes.

C - Do you want to pray right now?

N - Yes.

C - Let's pray.

The participants at MELF were encouraged to follow this dialogue presentation with university and high school students, as well as with adults and educated people. When sharing Christ with illiterate people, it was suggested that the diagram and explanation be simplified somewhat.

How to Become Spiritual Multipliers

Moving into the realm of follow-up and discipleship, the training sessions emphasized the biblical basis for follow-up of new converts on both an individual basis and in group settings. "Only the Holy Spirit can cause growth in a new believer," the seminar leaders stated, as they went on to point out the value of prayer, Bible study, church membership, fellowship with other believers, and sharing one's faith in the discipleship process. The three-fold process of spiritual multiplication (*winning* people to Christ, *building* them in their faith, and *sending* them out to win, build and send still others) which the apostle Paul outlines in II Timothy 2:2 was explained in depth, as a continuing cycle which should describe the growth of Christianity wherever believers exist.

In relation to these concepts, one of our guest speakers during the week identified a number of sensitivities to observe in winning and then discipling a Middle Easterner:

1. Accept and love him as your true friend.

2. Create an open atmosphere for discussion of spiritual matters within the privacy of your own home, away from his environment.

3. Be a model of faith and honesty for him to emulate.

4. Keep every secret that he may share with you.

5. Be sure that he knows the difference between institutional religion and personal faith.

6. Avoid arousing his fears and prejudices.

7. Encourage him to count the cost of becoming a disciple of Jesus Christ.

8. Introduce him to trusted and sensitive believers with whom he can fellowship.

9. Pray and read God's Word with him, relating both to his personal problems.

10. Encourage him to live a life in keeping with his profession of faith and to witness wisely to his family and friends.

Rural Strategies

Another entire seminar was devoted to a presentation of fresh strategies based on biblical principles which are now in use around the world for rural evangelism and discipleship in the developing nations. In essence, this involved ways to communicate the gospel and the basics of Christian growth to people in small village settings, most of whom cannot read. Since well over 60% of the people in the Middle East fall into this category, the entire Fellowship listened with keen interest and growing excitement to these plans.

As these various training sessions continued through the week of MELF, I began to sense a swelling undercurrent of expanded faith and vision among the delegates. It was dawning upon us all that we now had defined the basic training need of the church of Jesus Christ in the Middle East in regard to evangelism and discipleship. These simple, culturally relevant, scriptural concepts we had just reviewed provided a comprehensive foundation for every personal, church and cooperative effort of evangelism and discipleship that could be attempted in the months and years to come. The participants were so eager to try out this simple method of sharing the love of Christ that several times I saw one or more of them off to one side in the halls and lounges of our hotel, sharing a little Four Spiritual Laws booklet with a passerby.

A smile crept across my face every time I saw a MELF delegate taking out a Four Spiritual Laws booklet, forming the habit of sharing the love of Jesus Christ as a way of life. I recalled a letter received from an educated Muslim in Pakistan last year. As he thanked our staff for sending him an "I Found It!" booklet (the Four Spiritual Laws accompanied by personal testimonies of Pakistani believers), he commented very candidly, "I have read (it) carefully and with great interest. . . . It is hardly possible for any open-minded man to disagree with the Four Spiritual Laws. I am glad to learn that the Christian doctrine is based not only on feelings and emotions, but also on facts and reasoning faith!"

I was confident that, by God's grace, thousands upon thousands of other open-minded Muslims in the Middle East would hear the truth about the love of Jesus Christ through these MELF participants — and the multiplied witness of those they would train — back in their own nations.

CHAPTER
THIRTEEN

Applying a Kingdom Mentality

". . . New wine must be put into fresh wineskins."

Luke 5:38

"We should make plans that are so logical, but so supernatural — so far beyond our own ability — that God will get all of the glory! We should expect God to do something so great that people will say, as they look at us, 'They couldn't have done that — *God did it*!' "

It was the fourth night of the Middle East Leadership Fellowship, and Mr. Swede Anderson was whetting the participants' anticipation for the forthcoming training on biblical principles of management with his message on "Qualifications for the Supernatural Planner." As director of the Christian Embassy in Washington, D.C., Mr. Anderson rubs shoulders with diplomats from all over the world as well as with many U.S. government leaders. He came to this position after a number of years of international experience, including the responsibility of directing our ministry across the continent of Latin America. His close friendship with a former ambassador of Cyprus to the United States was one of many motivations that drew Mr. Anderson and his wife, Judy, to attend the MELF sessions in Nicosia.

Qualifications for the Supernatural Planner

Mr. Anderson's first three "qualifications" were drawn from the fifth chapter of II Corinthians, where the apostle Paul reveals the inner motivation which brought him to decisions affecting his entire life-style.

1. *Be convinced of Jesus' love for me.* "Our first qualification comes from verse 14," he began, "where Paul states, 'For the love of Christ controls us.' From the other two places where this same word 'control' or 'constrain' is used, we find out that Paul was saying that God's love *presses in upon us*, like a thronging crowd, irresistably controlling us, and that it *surrounds or encompasses us*, like a powerful army. By way of

114

application, this means that the supernatural planner is so convinced of this kind of great, overwhelming love that He trusts God in all circumstances. He is not afraid to present himself to God as a living sacrifice, as Romans 12:1,2 exhorts us to do, because he actively believes the tremendous promise of Romans 8:32, 'He who did not spare His own Son, but delivered Him up for us all, how will He not also with Him freely give us all things?' "

2. *Choose no longer to live for self, but for Christ.* "This decision was based on Paul's first conviction that Jesus loved him," declared Mr. Anderson. "He continues into verse 15 by saying, '. . . He died for all, that they who live should no longer live for themselves, but for Him who died and rose again on their behalf.'

"There is perhaps no choice that you will make in the course of your entire life that will more greatly release the freedom of God to work through you than the decision that you want Him to get *all* the glory in everything that happens in your life. No matter where we live, no matter what our culture might be, we are always tempted to reach in and take just a little of God's glory for ourselves. When we take any of the credit for ourselves, we are usually convinced that we really *do* have something to contribute! But when we come to the realization that we have nothing at all of value in ourselves, and that we must go to God to get everything from Him to pass on to others who come to us to have their needs met — then, and then only, will God bless us in abundance."

3. *Take the role of a servant in all situations.* "Paul had obviously learned to see people as Jesus saw them," Mr. Anderson continued. "He says in verse 16, 'Therefore from now on, we recognize no man according to the flesh. . . .' Take for an example the people who are physically near to us, but ethnically or culturally different from us. In my limited experience, I have yet to be exposed to any culture on the face of the earth in which Christians naturally believe that people like this around them are open to the gospel. So it is very easy for me to look at some person or group of people and list off a number of reasons why I should *not* talk to them about Jesus Christ. But the Scriptures teach a totally different point of view. Paul says that we are not to look at people through fleshly eyes, seeing them through the limitations that their culture (or ours) might have.

Instead, we look at everyone — the lost, the culturally or ethnically different, our brothers and sisters in Christ, and even our own wives or husbands — through the eyes of Jesus."

4. *Expect new structures, systems, activities and possibilities.* "In the fifth chapter of Luke," Mr. Anderson emphasized, "we learn that the Number One Problem on the face of the earth is sin and its forgiveness. We Christians know that Jesus Christ is the only solution to man's sin — but still, we will be tempted to believe that there are many other solutions to man's problems. Notice in Luke's story about Levi (Matthew) how Jesus dealt with the problem of sin.

"Ultimately, of course, Jesus dealt with sin by going to the cross, but in His daily dealings with people, we see that He went into the midst of the sinners! He went where they were. He ate with them. He had fun with them. He enjoyed their fellowship. He purposely went to be with them — and when He was rebuked for this, He replied, 'It is not those who are well who need a physician, but those who are sick. I have not come to call righteous men but sinners to repentance.' It is clear," Mr. Anderson stated, "that if you and I are going to follow the pattern that Jesus Christ established, and thus solve the Number One Problem on earth, *we must immerse ourselves in the midst of people who are yet unforgiven.*

"Jesus goes on to make a final analogy that reveals God's supernatural planning for this world. He says that everyone knows better than to put new wine in old wineskins, which would soon burst from the pressure. Instead, they put new wine in new wineskins. New wine is like new life in Jesus Christ, finding forgiveness and eternal life. Jesus said that you cannot put this new life in old wineskins. Old containers cannot contain new solutions.

"So I would urge you," Mr. Anderson concluded, "to keep this analogy of our Lord in mind as you go into the management and planning sessions on Monday morning. Open your mind before God, saying, 'Lord, there must be new systems, new containers, new habits, new attitudes, new structures, new ways of doing things that I've never thought of before — *new wineskins* that You want to fill through me, in order to bring new life to the people around me.' May we all open our minds to the possibility of God doing things we have never thought about before — of pouring new wine through us to bring His mighty solution to the world's Number One Problem: forgiveness of sins."

Ministry of Management

Three days later, we joined as a Fellowship to concentrate on two intensive days of interaction on the "Ministry of Management" in our personal lives and through our Christian ministries and churches. We were fortunate to have Mr. Steve Douglass, acknowledged as one of America's foremost authorities on the subject of Christian management, personally arrange his schedule and finance his own way to participate in these vital discussions. Mr. Douglass, who serves as vice president for administration with Campus Crusade, is co-author of *The Ministry of Management* and author of *Managing Yourself*. He has been largely responsible for placing the concepts of biblical management into a transferable structure now being shared around the world by our movement and many others. For a number of years he has been involved internationally in teaching Christian management seminars on every continent.

As the MELF delegates opened their notebooks to the section on management training, my mind went back to the first management seminar I had heard Mr. Douglass teach. I had been somewhat doubtful that his lectures and workshops would be all that beneficial to me, after my seminary training and several years of ministry experience. In my mind, when I heard the term 'management,' I pictured in my mind lots of charts and graphs and rather boring paper work, which I feared would regiment and even clutter up my ministry with people. But that was before Mr. Douglass began with his simple definition of what management is all about: "It's simply getting things done through other people!" he declared. Suddenly "the light came on" for me, and I was interested to learn about the role of management in my Christian life.

As Mr. Douglass began to introduce his subject before our Fellowship, I glanced around the conference room. From the delegates' expressions, I could see that many were experiencing the same relief and new enthusiasm I had felt, when I had first participated in this soundly biblical presentation. My satisfaction knew no bounds, for I realized they were being saturated with principles that were as intensely practical as they were profoundly scriptural.

We began with a look into God's Word: "Moreover it is required in stewards, that a man be found faithful" (I Corinthians 4:2, KJV). "Christians need to learn to manage well," Mr. Douglass explained, "because we are commanded to be good stewards of our time and abilities. The Bible gives us many good examples to follow, such as Joseph, Daniel and Paul." After examining the lives of these men of God, he proceeded into the four major steps of the management process: planning, organizing, leading and controlling.

1. *Planning (predetermining a course of action).*

> "For which one of you, when he wants to build a tower, does not first sit down and calculate the cost, to see if he has enough to complete it? Otherwise, when he has laid a foundation, and is not able to finish, all who observe it begin to ridicule him, saying, 'This man began to build and was not able to finish' " (Luke 14:28-30).

"Christians should lead orderly lives," Mr. Douglass emphasized, "because Christ advocated that we think ahead and move toward His chosen objectives. This is particularly true in Christian work of any kind, as shown to us in the example of the apostle Paul. When God gave Paul the objective to evangelize and disciple the Gentiles, Paul followed a clear plan. He began by preaching in synagogues or among interested listeners; he performed miracles as led by the Holy Spirit; he then established leadership groups to evangelize the community; and finally he selected a specific person among the believers to carry on the ministry after he had gone. Later he followed up his travels by letters. Every trip was for a special purpose, according to a definite plan. He chose strategic cities to visit, and as soon as the gospel took root, he moved on to the next place. What were the results? We read in Acts 19:10, 'All who lived in Asia heard the Word of the Lord.' This was total saturation of the area! God blessed Paul's efforts, for the greatest test of any plan is whether it works."

Mr. Douglass went on to explain in detail the five steps of good planning. "Begin with prayer, then establish your objectives. After you have made a program, listing every logical step necessary to fulfill your objectives, go on to set up a schedule and estimate your budget. Be sure that your plan is beyond what you can do in your own strength, according to I Corinthians 10:31, so that you are forced to trust God for it. Finally, you should remain sensitive to the Lord's leading, expecting that He may want to alter some of the details of your plan."

2. *Organizing (the process of placing people into a structure to accomplish objectives).*

> "God is not a God of confusion. . . . let all things be done properly and in an orderly manner" (I Corinthians 14:33,40)

"Organization, or the lack of it, can determine whether or not important things are accomplished for God's glory," declared Mr. Douglass. "It can also affect the efficiency, effectiveness and sense of fulfillment of all the people involved in carrying out these important things. In the Old Testament, Nehemiah exemplifies in a wonderful way the important principles of organization. Nehemiah decided on his strategy before he tried to organize the work of building the wall, and then he grouped everyone by family units for their tasks, giving definite assignments to all the people. As a result, he developed a balanced structure for accomplishing his objectives."

Mr. Douglass went on to explain the three major steps involved in good organization. *"Organizing from the plan* involves a careful working through of your plan — listing all the activities, identifying the natural groups, and preparing a simple chart to show the structure of working relationships between all of the people involved in accomplishing the plan. Then, *job descriptions* need to be agreed upon in detail for every person, so that each individual's job is clear to everyone involved. Finally, *delegation* is an essential, ongoing process through which those in leadership positions share their responsibilities with others. When leaders are faithful to do this, they will find, even as Moses did, that they lighten their own burdens, develop more responsible leaders and also increase the total amount of work accomplished — which brings more glory to God."

3. *Leading (causing people to take effective action).*

> "To aspire to leadership is an honorable ambition" (I Timothy 3:1, NEB).

"Certainly the apostle Paul exemplified the qualities of a good Christian leader," stated Mr. Douglass, as he shared with

Steve Douglass
teaches
management
principles.

Middle Eastern believers apply scriptural principles of management and planning to help fulfill Christ's Great Commission in their own countries.

Kundan Massey defines the fulfillment of the Great Commission in the Middle East.

us eight important "how to's" of leadership taught in God's Word:

1. Thoroughly believe in, be saturated with and radiate the objective God has given to you.

2. Live an exemplary, energetic, disciplined life.

3. Be able to think and willing to learn.

4. Be able to make and stick to decisions, despite tension and uncertainty.

5. Be confident and positively oriented.

6. Be a servant.

7. Learn how to empathize.

8. Realize that your security is in Christ.

"The apostle Paul also concentrated upon some very clear guidelines in motivating others toward leadership," our speaker continued. "It was to Timothy, one of his most promising disciples, that he gave the classic explanation of spiritual multiplication found in II Timothy 2:2: 'And the things which you have heard from me in the presence of many witnesses, these entrust to faithful men, who will be able to teach others also.' " All of these guidelines are again principles from God's Word:

1. Concentrate on making your disciple a self-starter.

2. Show him the needs through exposure to reality.

3. Convey enthusiasm.

4. Show him how.

5. Elicit specific commitment.

6. Provide encouragement and recognition.

7. Develop him.

8. Love and minister to him.

4. *Controlling (assuring that performance conforms to plan).*

"I want to suggest that you finish what you started to do a year ago, for you were not only the first to propose this idea, but the first to begin doing something about it. Having started the ball rolling so enthusiastically, you should carry this project through to completion just as gladly, giving whatever you can out of whatever you have. Let your enthusiastic idea at the start be equalled by your realistic action now" (II Corinthians 8:10,11, LB).

After reading this passage, Mr. Douglass explained, "The apostle Paul wrote these words to the church at Corinth because they were not following through with their plan made a year earlier to help meet some of the critical financial needs of the struggling church in Jerusalem. There had been much initial enthusiasm, but very little had actually been accomplished afterwards. Therefore," he continued, "we can see that this step of controlling is vital to sustain the momentum of any new project."

Mr. Douglass related three essential steps to follow in the control of our plans made for God's glory. "First, establish some 'standards of performance,' listing in explicit detail the conditions that will exist when the job is done acceptably. Then, measure the results periodically — find out what has happened in the implementation of the plan, and how the people involved have developed as a result. You will then be able to follow your final step — to either make any necessary corrections in your plan, or to motivate the individuals involved to fulfill the original plan."

Active Application

Around the dinner table after that first day of management training, I sensed that some basic concepts of planning and organization had "caught fire" among the MELF participants. The discussions and gestures were more animated than ever, as delegates talked in terms of application — "to my country," "to our church at home," "to my own life and ministry." Appropriately, I was scheduled that same evening to share with them a message that I had given many times before, on every major continent of the world. It was the first time in my life, however, that I had been impressed so strongly that to stand and deliver this message to my fellow believers in the Middle East was, literally, to put our lives on the line together for Jesus Christ.

As usual, I began by saying, "Tonight I want to share with you the greatest plan ever given to man, by the greatest Person who ever lived, concerning the greatest power ever revealed, with the greatest promise ever recorded. I refer to the Great Commission of our Lord Jesus Christ, as recorded in Matthew 28:18-20: 'All authority has been given to Me in heaven and on earth. Go therefore and make disciples of all the nations, baptizing them in the name of the Father and the Son and the Holy Spirit, teaching them to observe all that I commanded you; and lo, I am with you always, even to the end of the age.' "

A sea of faces before me, representing nearly every nation of the Middle East, seemed to mirror my own burden as I declared, "The Great Commission of our Lord was not some beautiful benediction. It was a command, a parting call to action from Jesus Christ before He ascended into heaven. Although it was spoken originally to the 11 disciples, it involves all Christians everywhere. It applies to each one of us here tonight."

Clarifying the Cause

By matter of definition, I explained, "Jesus makes it clear that His commission is to evangelize and disciple, not to Christianize. He commanded us to proclaim the gospel to all men everywhere and to make sufficient disciples everywhere to saturate every community with the gospel. I want to clarify that fulfilling the Great Commission in the Middle East does not mean that every person in the Middle East will hear the gospel and accept Jesus Christ! Nor does it mean that entire nations will be Christianized, nor even that a majority of Middle Easterners will understand how to become Christians.

"However, it *does* mean that the entire Middle East will be saturated with the message of Christ, so that the truth about Him will become common knowledge — in the same sense that everyone knows that Americans from the Apollo spaceship walked on the moon. It means that a sufficiently great percentage of people in the Middle East will have heard the gospel, so that Jesus has become an issue in every nation. An overwhelming majority, therefore, will have had opportunity to receive Jesus Christ. At the same time, there will be a sufficient number of Spirit-filled, loving, obedient disciples in each nation who are committed to the ongoing process of fulfilling the Great Commission in the next decade and the next, if Jesus tarries."

Reminding my fellow believers that the Great Commission was a command, not an option, I emphasized, "We should take the Great Commission seriously, because our Lord Himself commanded it, because men are lost without Christ and because men everywhere are hungry for God. Christ intended for His Great Commission to be fulfilled in every generation, because He would never assign us to an impossible task. For this reason, we as individual Christians, as churches, as Christian groups must find our God-given strategy to contribute to our maximum in God's overall plan to share His love with the whole world."

God's Idea

Anticipating their questions, I explained, "But you may be asking, quite honestly, '*How* will the Great Commission be fulfilled? Is there really a plan in the heart of God for saturating *my* country with the love of Christ?' Let me assure you that God does indeed have a plan. After all, the Great Commission is all God's idea! Jesus came to seek and to save the lost, and God's Word says that God is not willing that any should perish, but that all should come to repentance. So every believer and every church in the Middle East has a strategic role in God's overall plan to fulfill the Great Commission in this part of the world. It is our responsibility, as Spirit-filled believers, to ask God in faith to show us just what that role is.

"For example," I stated, "we in Lifeagape International have realized that we need a plan for our ministry, if we are to fulfill the vision God has given our movement to help fulfill the Great Commission here in the Middle East. Therefore, we have set some goals and established some target dates — all of which are totally impossible apart from the supernatural intervention of God! But we are moving out in faith, convinced that these strategies are part of God's overall plan to saturate the Middle East with His love.

"As an individual," I probed, "you need to have a personal strategy. You should plan out the ways in which you can personally be involved in fulfilling the Great Commission. These will probably revolve around a ministry of evangelism and discipleship as a part of your own local church. Of course, your church also needs a clear plan, a strategy to saturate your entire community or city with the gospel. In addition, every Christian organization working in cooperation with the church should be targeting its efforts on specific concentrations of people within the national population — students, civic leaders, minorities, illiterates, military personnel, children, villagers and every other group — in order to saturate every level of society with the love and message of Jesus."

Strategic Final Thrust

In conclusion, I stated, "Lifeagape International has sponsored this Fellowship because we believe that this is a strategic, unique time in all of history to trust God for the fulfillment of the Great Commission in the Middle East. We believe that today we face even fewer obstacles than the first-century Christians did. After all, they had no TV, no radio, films, tapes or printing presses — they had in a number of cases even less freedom of speech under the Roman Empire than we have today in our various countries.

"With all my heart," I admitted, "I believe that the next year and on into the decade of the '80's may be the final thrust for the saturation of the Middle East for Christ in our generation. You and I hold in our hearts the key to the fulfillment of our Lord's command in our countries. Are you ready to pray with me, 'Lord, do it again, as You did in the first century! Use me to help make Jesus Christ the issue in every home, the name on every tongue, the focus in our cities, our villages and this entire region!'

"Working together, we can reach every home, truly saturating the Middle East with the love of Jesus Christ. Working independently, we will have business as usual. Which will it be? I challenge you to begin today to get vitally involved in the most important challenge in 2,000 years, the fulfillment of Christ's Great Commission. If we in this room are obedient to do so, together, then we will release an opportunity for spiritual harvest that has never been seen before in the Middle East."

As I gave my closing challenge to the MELF delegates to stand as an indication of their holy commitment before God to help fulfill the Great Commission through their lives and witness, I was deeply moved. I felt tears coursing down my face, for God's Holy Spirit was working in a powerful way in many lives. Some leapt to their feet, and for others it was a struggle, but by God's grace nearly every participant made a strong, personal commitment that night to help fulfill the Great Commission.

Maximizing the Ministry

The next morning, to cap our sessions on biblical management, the staff member coordinating our Here's Life thrust in the Middle East discussed with the MELF delegates effective ways to maximize their ministry influence. "The heart's cry of every believer who knows the joy of the Spirit-filled Christian life is the prayer, 'Lord, use my life to the maximum,' " he declared.

Turning our attention to Like 10:1,2, he reminded us that our Lord's priority at the height of His ministry was the concept of *multiplying disciples.* "Jesus had 12 disciples," he related, "but here He appoints 70 others, and He goes on to command His followers to pray for even more laborers for the ripening harvest around them." With that principle in mind, he went on to mention many of the elements which must be maintained in good balance if a Christ-centered church or group is to see phenomenal, supernatural growth take place.

"The leadership must believe that God wants their church to grow, and they must be obedient to lead by example," he stated. "A vision for reaching people for Christ is *caught*, not taught. At the same time, you must set specific goals, both long-range and intermediate, and then be consistent to check your progress on those goals periodically. Time is one of our most valuable resources, so each individual as well as the group as a whole must evaluate his time priorities consistently."

Supernatural Implications

Their notebooks open once more, the MELF participants began to work through the implications of all they had digested in relation to planning, management and the fulfillment of the Great Commission. They thought and prayed for long moments over various worksheets and the MELF Impact Planning Sheet. In some of the workshops they worked silently on an individual basis, with only the sound of many pens moving rapidly across the pages. Later, they clustered in small national groups, outlining together their plans and dreams and visions for the literal fulfillment of the Great Commission among their own people.

Their expressions were serious, yet filled with awe and restrained excitement, for they were helping to put on paper for perhaps the first time in many centuries a "supernaturally realistic plan" to saturate their various nations with the loving claims of Jesus Christ. Ideas and possibilities that none of us had ever considered before in the Middle East began to flow, and I realized that the delegates had begun to draw upon the powerful perspective of another MELF message — Dr. Larry

Poland's address on "Lives Characterized by the Supernatural."

Dr. Poland, as director of The *Agape* Movement of Campus Crusade, is playing one of the most significant roles in the Christian world today to encourage trained western Christians to invest their skills and experiences in more undeveloped countries of the world. Because of his international heart, he left the presidency of an American Christian university to involve himself in a round-the-clock ministry of service to the Third World.

His enthusiasm and vision for a supernatural lifestyle were obvious as he began to speak. "I trust that these very deep convictions which I am going to share with you will cause us to lift our eyes above the circumstances here in the Middle East — above the minority mentality that we Christians are often tempted to have — to a way of thinking that I call a Kingdom Mentality. I define a Kingdom Mentality as an unshakable commitment to the sovereignty of Christ and to the growing establishment of an invincible and perfect world order.

The Jesus Revolution

"Let me explain what I mean. Some time ago on a plane, I encountered a lady who was a Marxist journalist. She talked so loudly about her philosophy and her beliefs that finally I could stand it no longer, and I began to ask her some questions. She soon got the idea she was being led into something, so she stopped me in the middle of a sentence and said, 'Just who are you, anyway, and what do you do?'

"Without blinking an eye, I said, 'I am an agent in the Jesus revolution, the only revolution that will eventually conquer the world.' I couldn't have stunned her more if I had punched her in the nose! She had probably not met many Christians who perceived themselves in this way, but this is how we *should* view ourselves. Royal blood flows in our veins. We are sons and daughters of the King of kings and the Lord of lords, and we don't have to apologize to anyone. We don't have to be defensive, to think ourselves weak or poor. We are sons of the Kingdom!"

Then Dr. Poland proceeded to share 10 observations on the Kingdom Mentality from Jesus' parables in Matthew 13:

1. The secrets of the Kingdom are granted only to believers.
2. Understanding and committing ourselves to the Kingdom and the sovereignty of Jesus Christ are factors in our spiritual survival.
3. The growth of the Kingdom parallels the growth of evil.
4. The growth of the Kingdom is tiny at first but enormous at maturity.
5. The impact of the Kindom will eventually saturate the whole world.
6. True believers are "sons and daughters of the Kingdom."
7. Christ's Kingdom is designed to reflect the radiance of the righteous.
8. Discovering the Kingdom destroys a man's involvement with the world.
9. The Kingdom-cause captures all kinds of people.
10. The disciple of the Kingdom has great treasures, both old and new, to share with others.

There were four valuable conclusions which Dr. Poland drew from these great truths about the Kingdom of God:

1. God has designed every human being to have a Kingdom Mentality.
2. The world has never been more ready for the message of the Kingdom.
3. A Kingdom Mentality is the only thing capable of waking Christians out of their apathy and of stealing momentum from the enemy.
4. To a world that is hungry for the Kingdom we dare not offer our religious 'system.'

Taking Faith Risks

In closing, he related an incident that happened on his first trip to the Middle East, as he discussed the spread of the gospel in this part of the world with some of the believers.

"Is there anybody who is risking his life to witness openly to Muslims?" he asked.

"Well, yes, a few," they answered, after some thought.

"Well, what's happening to them? Dr. Poland asked.

"They are being thrown in jail, and some are persecuted."

"Then what happens?" he pursued.

"Ummm, well," they said, "it makes the believers more bold, and others rise up to proclaim the Good News."

"And what happens to them?" Dr. Poland continued.

"Oh, they are thrown in jail and persecuted."

"But what happens to the gospel?"

"Oh," they admitted, "the gospel increases!"

"This is the kind of Kingdom Mentality that I see in the book of Acts," declared Dr. Poland. "I don't see any place where the first-century Christians prayed for safety, but I see a lot of places where they prayed for the boldness of the Holy Spirit as they went into the 'high risk' areas of their society. That was frightening. It was full of risks. But they did it, and the gospel took root and spread as a result.

"Do you realize," Dr. Poland demanded, "that there has never been a civilization yet that has been able to stop the gospel and the bearers of the gospel who had this kind of Kingdom Mentality? Until you and I have that kind of conquering world view through the power of God's love, I think we cannot expect much to happen here in the Middle East. But when we do, nothing — absolutely nothing — can stop us!"

In the closing days of MELF, as I talked in depth with our national participants from all across the Middle East, I realized that in our eight days together, God *had* given us this revolutionary Kingdom Mentality. For perhaps the first time in my lifetime, a representative group of Middle Eastern believers had agreed to abandon anything that hinted of a minority mentality, and together — as trained, Spirit-filled, believing followers of the King of kings — we were stepping out in faith toward the fulfillment of the Great Commission in every nation of the Middle East.

It was as if the words of our Fellowship's theme verse had come to life, leaping off the banners overhead which declared in Arabic, Urdu, Persian, Greek, French and English the strong promise of our Savior,

"With men this is impossible, but with God all things are possible!" (Matthew 19:26).

CHAPTER
FOURTEEN

Invincible Weapon of Love

*". . . Let us love one another, for love is from God. . . . If
God so loved us, we also ought to love one another."*
I John 4:7,11

"We are taking our prophetic role as people of God engaged
in the ministry," declared our speaker of the evening, the Rev.
Sam Habib of Egypt. I had anticipated this national brother's
address to the Middle East Leadership Fellowship ever since
he had agreed to clear his schedule to come. As a leading
evangelical author, theologian and minister in his own country, Rev. Habib is widely known and respected across the Arab
Christian world as a church leader who is involved in the
practical outworking of his faith. I had prayed expectantly that
God would speak in a significant way at MELF through this
humble leader's presence and his message on "Ministry
Characterized by the Supernatural."

As I had expected, he spoke directly to some of the recur-
ring problems of the church in the Middle East. "We have to be
as wise as serpents, as well as being gentle like doves," he
emphasized. "Since childhood, things have been engraved in
our minds, so that we are unwilling to help and love and reach
out to our Muslim friends. I think that our task is much larger
than approaching people for Jesus Christ. If we stop evangelizing, of course, we have stopped the gospel. There is no gospel
without evangelism. But let us think about a strategy for the
ministry, because we should be planning for the future. We
should do today what we ought to do today — but at the same
time we should build our plans for tomorrow."

"My friends," he stressed, "we must plan our ministry so
that we not only win whomever we can win today, but at the
same time also win the coming generations in a great harvest!
A love relationship will increase understanding, so if the
present generation is not won, the coming generation will be
ready."

Our speaker went on to consider the vital issue of *personnel*

131

as the first of three major aspects of Christian ministry. "As I see it in the whole Middle East," he said, "the great task and success of the coming 10 years is going to be the job of the lay men and women. I am not minimizing what pastors are doing, because I am a minister myself. But pastors are occupied at least half or even much more than half of their time with what I call pastoral business, and we have so few pastors anyway. The main task in reaching the Middle East will be done by lay men and women who will quit their jobs and take a major responsibility in the ministry. Let me say that God's supernatural power is not going to work without us. The Holy Spirit has come to work in us. Don't wait for some miracle to come from heaven — the miracle is going to happen in *us*, and *we* will be used to carry the miracle and do it.

"Did you get it?" he repeated. "Let me say it again: Any church that does not hand over a major part of its ministry to its lay leaders is going to have empty pews very soon! Any pastor that will not do so is preventing the lay leadership from the role God has appointed them to fill as ministers in their own place. To some of you here, I think the Holy Spirit is calling you to quit your secular jobs and get involved in the ministry — not as pastors, but as lay leaders, lay men or women in your own communities or even another place." The stillness was almost electric, and I joined in the speaker's prayer that "the finger of the Holy Spirit" would point very specifically to various delegates through this challenge.

"I hope that you will give me your ears," he continued, "as I say that Jesus Christ in His ministry gave a very solid and prominent place to the humanity of man. This is the second aspect of our ministry we will consider, that of *approach*. I call this the service of love. Jesus cared about the sick, the suffering, the hungry, the poor, the needy. Jesus was concerned about the totality of man, as human beings created by God. Do we care for people like that? Not only caring for them as people to be evangelized, but sharing our resources along with our message because we really care. We love them."

Then he told how the mayor of a certain village in his country had come to him one day. He was full of suspicion, wondering why a national team of Christian medical workers had given their free services to the villagers month after month.

"Why have you treated these hundreds of Muslims in our village?" he asked. "I have kept a count, and you have given medicines and treatment to more than 400 of our people. You have even paid all the bills, which has cost much money. What are you getting at?"

Our speaker had simply countered, "Aren't you happy that these people are being treated?"

"Yes, of course," he said.

"Are they happy that they are now enjoying good health?"

"Why, yes," he admitted, "of course they are."

"Then this is our concern," our speaker had replied. "We love you. Jesus loves *us*, and He has taught us to love *you*."

"He looked at me strangely," said our speaker, "but you see, he was just beginning to see what the love concept is all about. It takes a great deal of work to help people understand the concept of love. So we need to pour love into the lives of the people around us. In doing this, we must remember that Jesus established the church, but not as an end in itself. The Christian church is a bridge to help people come to Jesus. When it becomes an end in itself, it becomes an institution, and this destroys the whole meaning of Christianity. The church is a bridge, a medium through which we bring people to Christ."

To move into his third consideration in the ministry, that of *manner*, our speaker remarked, "There is a lot of talk in the Middle East about presenting Christianity through silence. This is often because of fear about the political situation in the area. However, it is wrong to present Christ through silence alone. We need to speak out, being as positive as possible. We don't want to attack — we want to be constructive. If we tell someone that his way or his book is wrong, communication will be broken in a minute. On the other hand, if we recognize the nuggets of truth hidden in the other man's scriptures, and respect them as they agree with God's Word, then we can build constructively from there.

"When we endeavor to understand and love others, refusing to be judgmental toward them, the Holy Spirit will work in their hearts to convict and rebuke them, winning them over. I recall one experience when a highly educated Muslim confessed to me that twice he had set up a 'test' to give me opportunity to rebuke him for his wrongdoings. When I did not, he found that his own conscience suffered greatly, and he came to ask me more about the Christian faith. We talked into the early hours of the morning, and finally he sighed, 'I can see what you believe!' How grateful I was that I had not broken communication with that man, and as a result, God's love and understanding had reached out to him through me."

He concluded his message with a summary point on the incarnation. "We are called, very simply," he said, "to be an example of God's love incarnate in Jesus Christ. To me, incarnation means that God has come to me where I am. Tonight I am calling you to the ministry of incarnation. Go to the people around you, where they are. Respect them, even when they are immersed in their sin. Give them compassion and love, bringing them to new life in Jesus Christ. You and I need to become God's love incarnate, crucified for the sake of others. Are we willing to be?

"When Jesus expressed His mission, He said, 'I have come that men may have life, and may have it in all its fullness' (John 10:10, NEB). People who are living without Christ have life without its fullness. Only those who have Jesus Christ have life with all its fullness. Let us, in all humility, ask God to make us His love incarnate, sharing life in all its fullness with the people around us."

Historical Context

Another Arab Christian leader spoke to our Fellowship on the subject of the "Current Mind of the Middle Easterner." In a detailed historical review, this Arab brother examined the historical contest of attitudes and interactions that has built up between Christians and Muslims through the centuries since the time of the prophet Muhammad.

In conclusion, he pled, "Let us learn from history. I have a great hope that the church is no longer the church of the Middle Ages. All that is happening in the church everywhere in the world really thrills my heart, because I think that we have learned from the past. We have learned that nothing will gain the world except the love of Christ, the sacrificial love which Christ taught us by giving His life for us on the cross. We have learned that the church must give her life for the world, like the first-century church which was martyred in order to gain the Roman Empire. Unless the church of today is ready to give her life for saving the world, then I think we are going to repeat again the unhappy happenings of the past."

The Problem of Love

Another message which meshed closely with the burden of our Arab brothers for a new, supernatural love was that of the Rev. Don M. McCurry, director of the Samuel Zwemer Institute in Pasadena, Calif. Through the Rev. McCurry's life experiences as a missionary in Pakistan for 18 years, he has discerned that Christians from both the West and the East lack God's *agape,* unconditional love for Muslims. In response to the compassion which God has given him for the Muslim world, he is directing a strategic training program to help equip and motivate Christians to share the love of Jesus Christ with those of Muslim background. Because the Rev. McCurry has become a tremendous personal friend and dear brother in the Lord to me over the years, I rejoiced that God did a miracle and provided the funds for him to come and invest one day of vital ministry among us at the Middle East Leadership Fellowship.

"Last month I was invited to New York," the Rev. McCurry began, following the Middle Eastern pattern of couching his message within a story. "My assignment was to explain to a group of individuals, including two leading Muslim theologians from the Middle East, why Christians are trying to win Muslims to Christ! I couldn't believe the fantastic opportunity that God was giving to me. After much thought and prayer, I put aside the idea of dialogue regarding all the things that Muslims and Christians agree on and disagree on, and I began with my testimony of how I found Christ as a 24-year-old medical student."

Our speaker's warm smile engulfed the whole Fellowship as he admitted, "I was in irreverent young man! I had made a check list of all known mental diseases, because I wanted to see if Jesus was crazy! But eventually, I was confronted with John 14:6, where Jesus says, 'I am the way, and the truth, and the life; no one comes to the Father, but through Me.' I began to discover that although Jesus was different, He was not crazy. My last question was, 'Would Jesus tell a lie?' As I studied the gospels, I slowly came to the conclusion that Jesus said the unusual things He did because He could not lie — He *is* the Way, the Truth and the Life.

"So I shared with that group in New York my own experience of discovering Christ's love. You see, I had been reading about the apostle Paul's conversion experience, which he relates in Galatians 2:20: 'I have been crucified with Christ; and it is no longer I who live, but Christ lives in me; and the life which I now live in the flesh I live by faith in the Son of God, who loved me, and delivered Himself up for me.' Those last words became very real to me — 'the Son of God, who loved me, and delivered Himself up for me.' You see, I didn't know I *wanted* to be loved. I had grown up as a very normal, aggressive, competitive American male. I was convinced that everyone in the world was selfish. I thought that people didn't mean it when they used the word 'love.' I was so cynical that I believed that even in marriage, love was a hollow word.

"But that night, as I read those words and the reality of Christ's love came home to me, I began to weep like a small child. I remember saying through my tears, 'At last I have found Someone who loves me for no other reason, except that He loves me! At last I have found Someone with whom I can start my life over.'

"At this point, I turned to my Muslim friends in New York and said, 'We are not trying to force you to enter some form of western Christianity. We simply want you to discover Jesus, in the same way that I did as a young medical student.' Then I went on to speak of Jesus of Nazareth, explaining that we were not coming to them in our own name, as representatives of a competing religious system. We were coming in the spirit and power and love of Jesus Christ."

Jesus Transcends Culture

Turning from his story, the Rev. McCurry pointed his remarks to our Fellowship. "I am beginning to understand that the question before us in the Middle East is this: Are we going to present Jesus Christ in the power of the Holy Spirit, or are we going to present some form of cultural Christianity that will turn people away from the very One we want them to meet?

"I think that Jesus Christ is above culture. He transcends and transforms every culture, so that the gospel can take root in every culture. In Revelation 5:9, where Jesus returns to give John a vision of things to come, it says that there will be 'men from every tribe and tongue and people and nation' in the new heaven and new earth. This means to me that Jesus was not going to stress uniformity — rather, He is interested in pure diversity! He wants the church to take itself into every cultural form, to be unique and diverse, to be something that is purely befitting to that cultural setting!"

Mentioning several incidents from his experiences in Pakistan, the Rev. McCurry illustrated that neither the national believer nor the western missionary can dare to substitute his own society for Christianity. "Jesus set the gospel free to grow in every culture when He declared, 'God is spirit, and those who worship Him must worship in spirit and truth' (John 4:24). He liberated the gospel for all time from every kind of cultural trapping so that it could grow in *every culture*, even in the Islamic cultures around us!"

Returning to his story in New York, he related, "I told my Muslim friends that we Christians only want them to discover who Jesus really is. I told them that He is mentioned 93 times in the Qur'an. He is called the Messiah, the Word of God, the Spirit of God. He healed lepers, He gave sight to the blind, He raised the dead, He created out of nothing, He ascended into heaven, and He is alive today. I told them, 'We want you to discover *that* Jesus, and we invite you to study the Injil to complete your picture of Who He really is.'

"Do you know what their response was?" he asked us. "One of these Muslim leaders stood up and spoke before the whole meeting. He said, 'Mr. McCurry, this is the first time in all of my life that I have ever heard a clear presentation of what you Christians are trying to do and why. I want to thank you.' And that was only the beginning of their very warm response.

"I believe that our friends in Islam throughout the world are hungry for a true experience of Jesus Christ. However, I do not think that they are seeing Jesus in our Christian cultural forms as Someone who is free to take root in their cultures. We need to participate with God in bringing the people around us to the saving knowledge of Christ. He is asking us to be willing to learn the ways of other peoples, and if need be to go and live in the middle of them.

The Samaritan Example

"Jesus taught His disciples in a very powerful way how to overcome prejudice," continued the speaker. "They had been taught to hate Samaritans, but Jesus walked them right through Samaria, talked to a wicked prostitute-kind of woman, and then stayed for three days, making His disciples eat out of dirty Samaritan dishes and sleep on dirty Samaritan beds! They could not get away from these people whom they had avoided all of their lives!

"You and I can not get away from the people around us whom we have formerly avoided. For 1,400 years, there has been nothing but bloodshed and wars between Christians and Muslims, and all of us have inherited prejudice. The truth is that we don't like Muslims — but the truth is that Jesus Christ loves Muslims! And the truth is that we are going to have to repent and humble ourselves before God and go out and live in the midst of a people that our history and our culture have told us are *not* to be trusted, should *not* be loved and *cannot* be evangelized. God is asking you and me to go to our knees and pray, to give ourselves to loving those who may not love us. The Muslims are starved for love from Christian people, and when they find someone who loves them, they respond. The truth is that many devout Muslims are willing to become followers of Jesus Christ, even if they may not be willing to join your church, to adapt to your cultural pattern of Christianity.

"It all comes back to that first question I asked myself, 'Who is Jesus Christ? Who is He really?' If we do believe that He is the Way, the Truth and the Life, then we must be willing to die to ourselves, allowing the love of Christ to flow through us. Our problem in reaching the Middle East is a problem of our hearts. Are we willing to change and to begin really loving our Muslim neighbors?"

The Spirit of God spoke to hearts once again that morning, and as one body, we fell onto our knees, acknowledging our lovelessness and pride which had hindered the free and effective flow of the gospel here in the Middle East. Many participants were in particular sobered by Mr. McCurry's warning that throughout history, when the people of God refused to reach the unregenerate people around them, those unreached people became the very agent of God's judgment upon His own people!

After this session, little groups all over the hall broke into humbled discussions, confessing to each other, "This is true. We do not love the Muslims." I heard such admissions from a number, but along with their conviction there was a searching, an appeal, a grasping for *how* to change. "How do we stop distrusting and begin building these bridges of love?" the delegates were asking.

With this building restlessness for a practical answer to this question, it was exciting to me when it soon became apparent that God's Spirit wanted us to adjust our already tight schedule to include Dr. Bright's liberating message on "How to Love by Faith." I could almost feel the anticipation of our delegates as they listened to his opening words.

The Missing Point of the Outline

"For years, as I spoke on the subject of love," Dr. Bright said, "I had a beautiful four-point outline:

"First, God loves us unconditionally.

"Second, we are commanded to love others — God, our neighbors, even our enemies.

"Third, we are incapable of loving others in our own strength.

"Fourth, we can love others with God's love.

"But as in the case of most sermons on love, something was missing. Then some years ago, in an early hour of the morning, I was awakened from a deep sleep. I knew that God had something to say to me. I felt impressed to get up, open my Bible and kneel to read and pray. What I discovered during the next two hours has since enriched my life and the lives of tens of thousands of others. I learned *how* to love. With this discovery, God gave me the command to share this wonderful truth with Christians around the world. In that life-changing time of fellowship with the Lord, I was given a fifth point for my sermon on love: *We love by faith.*"

As Dr. Bright proceeded to share his message on love, everyone in our Fellowship was intent, almost leaning forward in their seats as they waited for the final point, the vital "how to" of loving by faith.

"How do we make love a practical reality in our lives?" asked Dr. Bright at last. "How do we love? By making resolutions? By following self-imposed disciplines? No, we love by faith. Everything about the Christian life is based on faith. We love by faith, just as we received Christ by faith, just as we walk by faith, and just as we are filled with the Holy Spirit by faith.

"However," he continued, "if the fruit of the Spirit is love, we may logically ask if it is not enough to be filled with the Spirit. This will always be true from God's point of view, but it will not always be true in our actual experience. In Hebrews 11:6 we are reminded that "without faith it is impossible to please Him." Obviously there will be no demonstration of God's love where there is no faith.

"I would remind those who have difficulty in loving others that Jesus has commanded us to 'love each other as much as I love you' (John 15:12, LB). Therefore, we know that it is God's will for us to love. We also know that He would not command us to do something that He would not enable us to do.

"In I John 5:14,15, God promises that if we ask anything according to His will, He hears and answers us. Relating this promise to God's command, we can claim by faith the privilege of loving with His love. God has available for us an unending supply of *agape* — His divine, supernatural love. In order to experience and share this love, we must claim it by faith, trusting His promise that He will give us all that we need to do His will, on the basis of His command and promise.

"This principle is not new," Dr. Bright admitted. "It is 2,000 years old. But it was a new discovery to me that morning some years ago, and since that time to many thousands of other Christians with whom I have shared it. When I began to practice loving by faith, I found that problems of tension with other individuals seemed to disappear, often miraculously.

"I remember a problem I was having loving a fellow staff member," he related. "It troubled me. I wanted to love him. I knew that I was commanded to love him. Yet, because of certain areas of inconsistency and personality differences, it was difficult for me to love him. But the Lord reminded me of His command in I Peter 5:7 to cast this care on Him and love this man *by faith*. I did. When I claimed God's promise to take this care, and claimed God's love for him by faith, my concern was lifted. I knew the problem was in God's hands.

"An hour later," he continued, "I found under my door a letter from that very man, who had no possible way of knowing what I had just experienced. In fact, his letter had been written the day before. The Lord had foreseen the change in me. This friend and I met together that afternoon and had the most wonderful time of prayer and fellowship we had ever experienced together. Loving with God's love, by faith, had changed our relationship."

Dr. Bright went on to relate incident after incident of Christians around the world whose lives and ministries had been transformed when they had heard and understood this concept. Then he urged us, "Begin to love by faith yourself. Make a list of people whom you do not like, and begin to love them by faith. Apply the truths of I Corinthians 13 to each one of them and to yourself as well. Ask God to enable you to see yourself as He sees you. You have no reason to dislike yourself when your creator has already forgiven you and demonstrated His unconditional love by dying for you.

"Perhaps your boss, a fellow worker, your children or other relatives will be on your list. Pray for each one, asking the Holy Spirit to fill you with Christ's love for them. Try it on every one of your 'enemies' — everyone who angers you, who ignores you, who bores you, or who frustrates you. The next time you meet them, draw upon God's limitless, inexhaustible, overwhelming love for them by faith. Watch God work through you, using your smile, your words, your patience to express His love."

There were expressions of discovery all across the conference room, and I was to learn later from the evaluation sheets that this one message was counted the highpoint of MELF by many of the participants. In my heart, I claimed in a new and specific sense the promise of Jesus, "By this all men will know that you are My disciples, if you have love for one another" (John 13:35). Love, the I Corinthians kind of love, was the answer, both within the church of the Middle East, and through it — and as a body, the Middle East Leadership Fellowship had learned how to appropriate this most powerful of spiritual weapons, loving by faith.

CHAPTER
FIFTEEN

Of One Mind and Heart

*". . . Being of the same mind, maintaining the same love,
united in spirit, intent on one purpose."*
Philippians 2:2

"I feel that I have received a blessing here that I wouldn't have foregone for anything. Perhaps the greatest blessing has been to see one's place in the great overall plan that God has for this world."

Our speaker was well known and respected, a pastor and Christian worker in the Arab world for more than 50 years. As a dedicated missionary who has immersed himself in the Arabic language and culture, he deserved his introduction at the Middle East Leadership Fellowship as "our American Arab brother in Christ." I was intrigued by his response to the many reports that were shared throughout the MELF sessions from across the Middle East, as well as from Africa, China and other parts of the world.

"As I hear all these reports of what God is doing here and there," he stated, "I realize that we are indeed in the last days. It seems to me that if one of the signs of the end of the age is that the gospel should be preached to all nations as a witness, then we are pretty near the end. But there is something, something that still remains in God's program, that has to sweep the Middle East.

"The gospel went out from the Middle East to start with," he continued. "It's gone right around the world, and now it's got to come right back to the Middle East, in the same power with which it started. So we can believe that even the most closed countries are being opened to the gospel, by God's grace.

"The Arab farmers, as you know, talk about sowing on dry ground. They sow the seeds, and then they wait for the rains to come. It seems to me that this is what we have been doing with the gospel in the Middle East — sowing it in faith upon dry ground, believing that when the rain of the Spirit comes, there will be a tremendous harvest."

Asserting that this harvest had already begun, he shared an account that a sheikh in a leading mosque of the Arab world had confided in him. This religious leader had just seen a vision of an unknown man appearing to him in his dreams.

"Who are you?" asked the sheikh.

"I am the Lord Jesus," replied the man, "and I am coming soon to solve all of your problems."

Our speaker asked the sheikh, "Do you have a Bible?"

In astonishment, the sheikh demanded, "Do you think I haven't got a Bible after *that*?"

Our elderly speaker went on to relate many other specifics of how God is working in the Arab country where he has lived and ministered for so many years. He finally concluded, "Now the time has come for a fresh momentum. The time has come for a new understanding of what spiritual Christianity means. Everywhere God is working, but we have to uncover what He is doing, and it should be blazed abroad!"

Call to Cooperative Unity

My heart lifted at his words, because I also felt that the time had come for a bold uncovering of the work of the Holy Spirit across the Middle East. It was for that reason I had devoted a major portion of my keynote address to a call for a deep spiritual level of unity and cooperation among all the believers of the Middle East. Through all of my years of ministry and experience in this part of the world, I had become convinced that only through such scriptural unity would holy boldness begin to characterize the thrust of the national believers, even though they were few in number.

In relation to small numbers, I reminded the delegates that God's Word records a wonderfully encouraging story of 300 men whose success in battle was characterized by the supernatural. In the seventh chapter of Judges, we are told that although 32,000 soldiers were available, Gideon was instructed to select from them a small group of only 300. It must have been difficult for Gideon to follow those instructions, because he and his people faced an allied army as thick as locusts. As a result, God's people were very frightened and fearful, not really trusting in the power of God. But Gideon obeyed God, and through this small company of "just 300 men," God displayed His invincible power for all men to see.

Notice that these 300 men really had very simple, commonplace equipment put into their hands for this great battle. Each one was given a trumpet, an earthen pitcher and a torch — all ordinary, inexpensive vessels which could be found anywhere in that locality.

But the most important thing is how they used these simple tools. God's Word tells us that all 300 men obediently waited for the signal from Gideon on what to do. When it came, they blew their trumpets in one united blast, they smashed their pitchers in one united action, and they raised their torches in one united thrust. This small band of men had committed themselves to act in unity, and in so doing they fulfilled the Lord's promise to Gideon, "Surely I will be with you, and you shall defeat Midian *as one man*" (Judges 6:16). They were 300 individuals, and all of them were used to doing things their own way, but they chose to act together, as one man.

One Banner of the Cross

We in the Middle East need to follow the example of Gideon and his men. We must act in unity to blow our trumpets, proclaiming God's truth of the gospel. We must act in unity to break any earthen or carnal parts of our lives and ministries which are hindering God's purposes. And we must act in unity to hold aloft Jesus, the Light of the world, letting the fire of the Holy Spirit burn brightly through our lives.

We all know how outnumbered we are here in this vast area of the Middle East. Less than 1,300 missionaries and national Christian workers are laboring through various churches and organizations in this whole area. That means one Christian worker per 170,000 people! Yes, we are a very, very small minority within a very great majority. And although we all have a common goal, we have been blowing our own trumpets in our own ways!

Unity was the secret of Gideon's success over that vast army, and I believe that unity is the only way we can accomplish our goal. I am not talking about organizational unity, but a much deeper unity — the unity of the Holy Spirit. We must be willing to pull down our little individual banners that promote our own denominations or organizations, and instead to thrust up the banner of the cross of our Lord Jesus Christ before all the peoples of the Middle East.

When the Holy Spirit accomplishes that work in our lives, the fact that we are few in number will become unimportant. There was once a courageous young man named Jonathan who told his armor bearer, "The Lord is not restrained to save by many or by few" (I Samuel 14:6). In that spirit, the two of them went on to lead an incredible victory for the Lord. Unity — a miraculous oneness of mind, heart and spirit — was the key to their success, as it will be to ours here in the Middle East.

Let us be realistic. The Muslim world is hard. The situation is serious, even critical. Circumstances are most unfavorable. But God's power, characterized by the supernatural, is "the same yesterday, today and forever" (Hebrews 13:8). I believe that God in His grace has permitted the Middle East Leadership Fellowship to become reality to help equip the Middle Eastern believers with renewed vision, solemn determination and a vital catalyst toward unity in the bonds of Christ's love.

The time is *now* for harvest here in the Middle East. We all know that harvest cannot wait. Now is the time for us to blow our trumpets in unity, to destroy anything in our lives that quenches the light and power of the Holy Spirit, and to lift high the torch of our Lord Jesus Christ. Before God, now is the time to take a step of faith for the Middle East. As Jesus Himself told us, "Night is coming, when no man can work" (John 9:4).

A Team 200 Strong

When the closing session of our Fellowship came, it was clear that our 214 registered participants were ready "as one man" to take that step of faith. More than a dozen delegates came privately to me or to our MELF director to inquire, "Could you conduct a MELF back in my country?" That in itself was confirmation that God had supernaturally achieved our objectives for the Fellowship! We were quick to explain to them that trained nationals from their own country, or a nearby country in the same language group, were fully prepared to present the same training and conference content. This could be presented as a whole, or in specific units such as Prayer Workshops, Management Conferences, Lay Institutes for Evangelism, etc. On a limited basis, outside speakers like myself could arrange to participate in such "mini-MELF's" where it was advisable for us to do so.

One after another, participants shared how God had spoken to their hearts during the Fellowship. One layman announced that God was leading him to leave his business and enter full-time Christian work as a layman. An Arab physician who was directing two busy medical clinics in his country stated that every day at MELF God kept telling him, "Return back to evangelism! Return back to evangelism!" He confessed through his tears that he was going to be obedient once again to give evangelism priority over his profession. Another participant volunteered, "I have learned how to channel my life and service for Christ in a disciplined way."

One relatively isolated believer wrote on the evaluation sheet, "I frequently felt alone and therefore an ineffective instrument. Now I see myself as a member of a team at least 200 strong!" A leading Pakistani pastor stood before the Fellowship to confess, "The Lord has used MELF to bring me to tears — tears of joy, of thanksgiving and of shame." One participant summarized the remarks of dozens of others when he said, "Dr. Bright's messages have shaken all my fake Christian pride."

Unprecedented and Strategic

Dr. Bright himself made some very strong, positive observations about the significance of the Fellowship as it drew to a close. In part, he commented: "This was an unprecedented, historic gathering of Middle Eastern Christians. It was without question the most significant gathering for strategic planning in how to reach the Middle East for Christ in this century, if not in the history of Christianity. I am confident personally that this Fellowship will be considered a watershed between belief and unbelief for the believers of the Middle East. And I pray that it will be the springboard for a great acceleration of prayer, evangelism and discipleship throughout this strategic part of the world.

"I believe," he declared, "that the Middle East Leadership Fellowship has become a very strategic instrument in the hand of God to help accelerate the fulfillment of the Great Commission in the Middle East. It is clear that if the Great Commission is not fulfilled in the Middle East, then it is not fulfilled around the world. Therefore, as world Christians, we need to reprioritize Christian manpower, finances, prayer and strategic planning to accelerate the cause of Christ in the Middle East.

We must ask God to provide supernaturally so that the goals that He has placed in our hearts will be reached.

"I am more persuaded than ever," he told the delegates at the closing banquet, "that through the enabling of God's mighty Spirit, we are going to see a great movement of God sweep across the Middle East. You who are here in this room tonight, along with all those who represent our Lord Jesus Christ throughout your countries, could well be the sparks to ignite that great light, illumining the people of the Middle East who have been darkened for so many long centuries."

With simple eloquence, Dr. Bright had voiced the passion of my own heart. As the last event of our last session together, we joined in a symbolic candle-lighting service that expressed our united commitment to Jesus, the Light of the world. In the darkened room that evening, Dr. Bright lit my candle, and then I turned to light the candles of each of our national directors. Within a few moments, as they in turn lit the candles near them, the light had spread quickly across the entire room. Hardly an eye was dry as we asked God to make this symbol come true, in spiritual reality, in every nation represented.

"The Middle East Leadership Fellowship is not over," I reminded them at that holy moment. "It has, in fact, just begun."

Four Eloquent Pictures

I reminded them of the poignant challenge I had met them with on the first evening of the Middle East Leadership Fellowship. In keeping with Middle Eastern tradition, my challenge was put indirectly, through a story of four pictures printed side by side in a magazine. Although my challenge was first directed to the national Christian leaders of the Middle East, I believe that it also applies to every reader of this book.

The first picture was of a vast wheatfield. From horizon to horizon, as far as you could see, there was a continuous landscape of wheat in every direction. And, in the middle of that great field of wheat, there was a small farmhouse.

The second picture was of that same vast wheatfield, but in the foreground there was a father, a mother and a few neighbors. One was going this way, one was going that way, one going another way. You see, there was a little boy who had wandered out of that farmhouse and into the great wheatfield, and they couldn't find him. So the second picture showed the parents and a few neighbors scattered throughout that great field, searching for the little boy.

The third picture was an exciting picture of action and movement, for it showed all of the family, friends and neighbors in that whole countryside joining hands together. With hands clasped in a great, long line, they were sweeping that field from side to side, trying to find the lost little boy.

And the fourth and last picture was one of the saddest pictures you could ever see. The last picture showed the father, standing over the dead body of his little son, looking down. Underneath the picture were the words, "Oh, that we had joined hands sooner!"

It is these same pictures that are being painted here in the Middle East today. In relation to reaching the Middle East for Christ, we are in the midst of a vast wheatfield, and even though we know that the people around us are lost, we are all going in different directions. We want to help them, but we are wasting valuable time because we have not agreed upon any plan to work together. It is the prayer of my heart that before it is too late, we will all join our hands in a common determination and dedication to bring the Lord Jesus Christ, the only hope of the world, to the lost people of the Middle East.

Will *you* join hands with us? Only God Himself can give you the courage and faith to believe Him to accomplish the supernatural in one of the most historically impenetrable regions of the world. And yet, I believe that we stand on the very threshold of a remarkable wave of miracles here in the Middle East. The people of Islam are hungry to know God in a personal way — and whether they remain in the village of their birth, or pursue their educational and business interests in the nations of the western world, they are amazingly open to the message and Person of Jesus Christ.

I invite you to join hands with the staff of Lifeagape International and the committed believers in the Middle East for a cooperative thrust toward the fulfillment of Christ's Great Commission in this neglected area. Through your believing prayers, your faithful stewardship and even your first-hand involvement with us here in the Middle East, you can have a strategic part in helping to tumble down the ancient barriers which have surrounded the Islamic peoples for 1,400 years.

I must warn you that a compassion for the Middle East may demand a great deal of you. It may cause you to cry out to God in agony of heart, even as Jesus wept over the city of Jerusalem for its stubborn resistance to His message. It may lead you to fast and pray in the spirit of Esther, who went on to intercede for her people at the risk of her own life. It may bring you to your knees with Isaiah, declaring, "Here am I, Lord; send me!" It may indeed cause you to follow Jesus back to the lands where He lived on this earth, to proclaim to the people of our generation in the Middle East the astounding Good News of the cross and resurrection of Jesus Christ.

But whatever the cost, I assure you that a holy compassion for the Middle East will cause your life to be characterized by the supernatural. Today Jesus is still saying, as He once declared in the hills of Judea, "With men this is impossible, but with God all things are possible."

Join hands with the believers of the Middle East in one of the most supernatural adventures in history: the fulfillment of our Lord's Great Commission among the Islamic peoples of the world in our generation!

APPENDIX I

DOCTRINAL SUMMARIES

In the five doctrinal summaries which follow, I have attempted to explain in layman's terms the background of Muslim perspective on certain essential Christian doctrines. I have chosen to limit this discussion to the five most common questions which Muslims have asked me over the years in their attempts to understand the Christian faith:

1. Has the Bible been changed?
2. Do Christians worship three gods?
3. Why do Christians call Jesus the "Son of God"?
4. Did Jesus really die on the cross?
5. How can a person experience forgiveness of sins?

Along with the historical background which has channeled the thinking of Muslims on these issues, I have mentioned a few passages from the Qur'an which may be used as positive bridges for thought when explaining the Christian faith in relation to that particular doctrine. Each summary then concludes with a brief outline of the teaching of the Word of God concerning that doctrine.

I have learned during the past 25 years that my demonstration of sincere respect for my Muslim friends and their beliefs is essential if I desire to see the gospel of Jesus Christ penetrate their minds and hearts with loving power. For that reason, I do find that occasional references to the Qur'an provide a helpful bridge from an individual's initial beliefs to the truths revealed in God's Word.

It is very probable that even those who live in the western world will have opportunity to share the love of Jesus Christ with individuals of Muslim background. It is my prayer that these doctrinal summaries will provide a helpful understanding "so that you may know how you should respond to each person" (Colossians 4:6), "yet with gentleness and reverence" (I Peter 3:15).

SUMMARY #1 — *HAS THE BIBLE BEEN CHANGED?*

A. The Muslim Perspective

One of the basic stumbling blocks in any discussion of the Christian faith in the Islamic world is the centuries-old conviction that Christians have changed the Bible. This major misunderstanding is the source of most of the other hindrances which a Muslim experiences in coming to a positive understanding of Christianity. Once a person accepts the Bible as the authentic, unchanged Word of God, however, then he is obligated by the teachings of the Qur'an to accept what God's Word teaches on the virgin birth, the trinity, the crucifixion and resurrection, forgiveness of sins and many more doctrinal truths.

During the lifetime of the prophet Muhammad, who lived some 600 years after the earthly life of Jesus Christ, the entire Bible as we have it today was available in complete written form. Throughout the Qur'an, the prophet Muhammad insists that not only the Qur'an but also the Injil (Gospels), the Torah (Law of Moses) and the Zabur (Psalms of David) are the authentic Word of God given by God Almighty Himself. The following references are a few of the many clear affirmations in the Qur'an that the prophet Muhammad accepted the inspiration of the Bible as it existed during his day:

"He (Allah) hath revealed unto thee (Muhammad) the Scripture with truth, confirming that which was (revealed) before it, even as He revealed the Torah and the Gospel" (Surah 3, *Al-i-'Imran*, The Family of Imran: 3).

"Say (O Muslims): We believe in Allah and that which is revealed unto us and that which was revealed unto Abraham and Ishmael, and Isaac, and Jacob, and the tribes, and that which Moses and Jesus received, and that which the Prophets received from their Lord" (Surah 2, *Al-Baqarah*, The Cow: 136).

"Lo! We did reveal the Torah, wherein is guidance and a light. . . . And We caused Jesus, son of Mary, to follow in their footsteps, confirming that which was (revealed) before him, and We bestowed on him the Gospel wherein is guidance and a light, confirming that which was (revealed) before it in the Torah" (Surah 5, *Al-Ma'idah*, The Table Spread: 44, 46).

"Lo! We inspire thee as We inspired Noah and the prophets after him, as We inspired Abraham and Ishmael and Isaac and Jacob and the tribes, and Jesus and Job and Jonah and Aaron and Solomon, and as we imparted unto David the Psalms" (Surah 4, *An-Nisa*, Women: 163).

Therefore, since the prophet Muhammad speaks with such reverence about the authority of the Torah, Zabur and Injil as the Word of God given from heaven, it is incumbent upon all devout Muslims to respect and believe these Scriptures. Not once does the Qur'an refer to the changing of these inspired books, so it is clear that the prophet Muhammad considered the Bible of his own day to be pure and undefiled. The Qur'an also speaks highly of the People of the Scripture (both Jews and Christians) "who recite the revelations of Allah" (Surah 3, *Al-i-'Imran*, The Family of Imran: 113), commanding them, "And believe in that which I reveal, confirming that which ye possess already (of the Scripture) . . ." (Surah 2, *Al-Baqarah*, The Cow: 41).

So it is clear that from the very beginning of Islam, the prophet Muhammad accepted the Bible as the unchanged, true Word of God. Because of his repeated instructions throughout the Qur'an to honor the People of the Book and their Scriptures, no Muslims after the time of Muhammad would have allowed any changes in the Bible, as the holy Word of God. Today there are two complete manuscripts of the New Testament which were written in Greek approximately 300 years before the time of the prophet Muhammad. The existence of these manuscripts, the Codex Sinaiticus and the Codex Vaticanus, indicates that the Word of God has not been changed, for it is the same today as it was 300 years before the Qur'an was written!

Furthermore, the Qur'an says repeatedly that God Almighty protects His Word from change: "There is no changing the Words of Allah" (Surah 10, Jonah: 64). "And recite that which hath been revealed unto thee of the Scripture of thy Lord. There is none who can change His words . . ." (Surah 18, *Al-Kahf*, The Cave: 27).

In light of this, even a devout Muslim must admit that he has no answers to the simple questions which are appropriate to ask of any person who claims that the Bible has been changed:

1. When could it have been changed?
2. Who would have dared to change it?
3. Where has it been changed?

B. The Christian Response

The Holy Bible, the inspired Word of God Almighty, is the Christian's final authority. As a divinely inspired textbook for man's spiritual life, the Bible remains unchanged and entirely consistent in its teachings, even though it was written over a period of 1,500 years through many Old Testament prophets and New Testament writers who were inspired by the Holy Spirit of God. Hundreds of very detailed prophecies contained in the Bible have already been fulfilled in miraculous ways, and even now we are seeing the fulfillment of many prophecies concerning the last days. As a result of scientific discoveries and archaeological excavations, historical evidence continues to verify the amazing, exact details of history which are portrayed in the Bible. At the same time, we find woven throughout the pages of God's Word the commands of God, the promises of God and, above all, the love of God for His creation.

The entire Old Testament was given to Moses and other prophets by God so that His people would live according to its commands and principles: "And these words, which I am commanding you today, shall be on your heart; and you shall teach them diligently to your sons and shall talk of them when you sit in your house and when you walk by the way and when you lie down and when you rise up" (Deuteronomy 6:6,7). David the Psalmist affirmed, "Forever, O Lord, Thy Word is settled in heaven" (Psalm 119:89). God declared through the prophet Isaiah, "So shall My word be which goes forth from My mouth; it shall not return to Me empty, without accomplishing what I desire, and without succeeding in the matter for which I sent it" (Isaiah 55:11).

In the New Testament, Jesus Christ again declares the authority of God's Holy Word: "Do not think that I came to abolish the Law or the Prophets; I did not come to abolish, but to fulfill. For truly I say to you, until heaven and earth pass away, not the smallest letter or stroke shall pass away from the Law, until all is accomplished" (Matthew 5:17,18). In another instance, Jesus said, "Heaven and earth will pass away, but My words will not pass away" (Luke 21:33), thus verifying the inspiration of His own teachings.

Many other passages in the New Testament reveal the clear inspiration of the Bible as the Word of God. "All Scripture is inspired by God and profitable for teaching, for reproof, for correction, for training in righteousness" (II Timothy 3:16). The Holy Spirit declares through the book of Hebrews, "For the Word of God is living and active and sharper than any two-edged sword, and piercing as far as the division of soul and spirit, of both joints and marrow, and able to judge the thoughts and intentions of the heart" (Hebrews 4:12).

Because the entire Bible is alive and active, no one has dared to change it through the centuries. Another clear proof of its inspiration by the Holy Spirit is the fact that the Bible continues to change thousands of lives around the world in positive, tangible ways. God's inspired Word is the same today as it was in the time of the Old Testament prophets and the New Testament apostles. The Bible is therefore our final authority, and we accept its teachings, commands and promises as they relate to all of life.

SUMMARY #2 — DO CHRISTIANS WORSHIP THREE GODS?

A. The Muslim Perspective

Islam came into being in the seventh century A.D. as a reaction against polytheism. Dismayed by this pagan worship of many gods which was prevalent all around him, the prophet Muhammad emphasized that there was only one true God, beginning the Muslim confession of faith with the words, "There is no God but Allah . . ."

Consequently, the Christian concept of the trinity of God implies to the Muslim the pagan worship of several gods. This is blasphemy, the unforgivable sin called *shirk*, to place any person equal with God in worship. Most Muslims assume that because Christians worship the Father, the Son and the Holy Spirit, they are worshiping in fact three gods. (Actually, due to the excessive emphasis upon Mary as the "Mother of God" during the prophet Muhammad's time, the Qur'an (in Surah 5,

Al-Ma'idah, The Table Spread: 116) substitutes Mary, the mother of Jesus, for the Holy Spirit, as the third person of the trinity.)

The standard text to which Muslims point in the Qur'an on this subject is addressed to Christians themselves: "O People of the Scripture! Do not exaggerate in your religion nor utter aught concerning Allah save the truth. The Messiah, Jesus son of Mary, was only a messenger of Allah, and His word which He conveyed unto Mary, and a spirit from Him. So believe in Allah and His messengers, and say not "Three" — Cease! (it is) better for you! — Allah is only One God. Far is it removed from His transcendent majesty that He should have a son. His is all that is in the heavens and all that is in the earth" (Surah 4, *An-Nisa*, Women: 171).

However, it is interesting to observe in this passage and a number of others that the Qur'an mentions the triune evidences of the one true God. The title of "Kalimat-Allah" (Word of God) is reserved for Jesus alone, and two terms, "Ruh-Allah" (Spirit of God) and "ar-Ruh al-Qudus" (Holy Spirit), are used for the Spirit of God. Such is the case in the following references:

"We gave unto Jesus, son of Mary, clear proofs (of Allah's sovereignty), and We supported him with the holy Spirit [*ar-Ruh al-Qudus*]" (Surah 2, *Al-Baqarah*, The Cow: 87).

"When Allah saith: O Jesus, son of Mary! Remember My favour unto thee and unto thy mother; how I strengthened thee with the holy Spirit [*ar-Ruh al-Qudus*], so that thou spakest unto mankind in the cradle as in maturity; and how I taught thee the Scripture and Wisdom and the Torah and the Gospel. . . . and thou didst heal him who was born blind and the leper by My permission; and how thou didst raise the dead, by My permission" (Surah 5, *Al-Ma'idah*, The Table Spread: 110).

"Go, O my sons, and ascertain concerning Joseph and his brother, and despair not the Spirit of Allah [Ruh-Allah]" (Surah 12, Joseph: 87).

"(And remember) when the angels said: O Mary! Lo! Allah giveth thee glad tidings of a word [*Kalimat*] from Him, whose name is the Messiah, Jesus, son of Mary, illustrious in the world and the Hereafter, and one of those brought near (unto Allah)" (Surah 3, *Al-i-'Imran*, The Family of Imran: 45).

Note that the above quotations from the Qur'an make reference to God, to His Word and to His Spirit. The Muslim who examines these references carefully can agree that the Qur'an does indeed teach him to believe in the Word of Allah and the Spirit of Allah, as well as in Allah the Almighty. So, in essence, because the devout Muslim accepts Kalimat-Allah (the Word of God) and Ruh-Allah (the Spirit of God) as taught in the Qur'an itself, he can accept the Christian doctrine of the trinity as accurately defined.

B. The Christian Response

According to the teaching of the Word of God, the one true God exists in three different ways or manifestations. Reference is made at the close of one of the New Testament epistles to "the grace of the Lord Jesus Christ, and the love of God, and the fellowship of the Holy Spirit" (II Corinthians 13:14), and in another passage the Holy Spirit declares, "For there are three that bear record in heaven, the Father, the Word, and the Holy Spirit, and these three are one" (I John 5:7, KJV).

The doctrine of one God is taught repeatedly throughout the Old and New Testaments. God spoke through Moses, "To you it was shown that you might know that the Lord, He is God; there is no other besides Him. . . . The Lord is our God, the Lord is one!" (Deuteronomy 4:35, 6:4). God inspired the apostle Paul to write, "For there is one God" (I Timothy 2:5), and in another epistle it is explained, "[There is] one God and Father of all who is over all and through all and in all" (Ephesians 4:6). When Jesus was being tempted by Satan, He declared, "Begone, Satan! For it is written, 'You shall worship the Lord your God, and serve Him only' " (Matthew 4:10).

At the same time, we find interwoven along with this doctrine the truth that the one true God is triune in His nature. In the Old Testament, God appeared to Noah, Abraham and many other prophets in different ways. Sometimes God appeared in fire, and other times He appeared as the Angel of the Lord or a "still small voice." Each time such a reference appears, God's Word makes it clear that this was a manifestation of God Himself.

Jesus Christ verified a number of times that He was one with God the Father. He stated, "I and the Father are one" (John 10:30) and "He who has seen Me has seen the Father" (John 14:9). The same truth is repeated in the epistle to the

Hebrews: "God, after He spoke long ago to the fathers in the prophets in many portions and in many ways, in these last days has spoken to us in His Son, whom He appointed heir of all things, through whom also He made the world. And He is the radiance of His glory and the exact representation of His nature, and upholds all things by the word of His power" (Hebrews 1:1-3).

We find a clear definition of the meaning of the Word of God at the beginning of John's gospel: "In the beginning was the Word, and the Word was with God, and the Word was God. . . . And the Word became flesh, and dwelt among us, and we beheld His glory, glory as of the only begotten from the Father, full of grace and truth. . . . No man has seen God at any time; the only begotten God, who is in the bosom of the Father, He has explained Him" (John 1:1,14,18).

One characteristic of a word is that it comes from one mind and communicates to another without really leaving the original mind. The word and the mind which sent it are one. In the same way, the light of the sun and the sun itself are one. The light comes to the earth and lightens it, but it is not separated from the sun. These are limited illustrations of how Jesus Christ came to the world as the Word of God without becoming separated from God.

It is not possible for our finite minds to prove or explain the supernatural, triune nature of God through comparisons to limited physical elements. But I have found the following three illustrations very helpful to those of Muslim background who need a logical frame of reference through which they can comprehend this concept:

1. The logical inquirer will often try to represent the doctrine of the trinity through a sum of addition:

1 God the Father + 1 God the Son + 1 God the Holy Spirit = 3 Gods

However, we can come much closer to the truth by following the process of multiplication, because $1 \times 1 \times 1 = 1$.

2. The formula called H_2O is only one substance, but it can appear in three different forms — steam, water and ice.

3. One man can fulfill three different roles or relationships — as a son to his father, a husband to his wife and a father to his own son. He is only one individual, yet at the same time he is a son, husband and father.

SUMMARY #3 — *WHY DO CHRISTIANS CALL JESUS THE "SON OF GOD"?*

A. The Muslim Perspective

While Christians would consider John 3:16 to be one of the most beautiful and concise statements of the central truths of the Christian gospel, this reference to Jesus as the only begotten Son of God brings offensive connotations to the mind of a Muslim. Since the time of the prophet Muhammad, Muslims have misunderstood this term "Son of God" to mean that Jesus was God's Son through physical sonship, as a result of a physical relationship between God and Mary. Although such an idea is as repugnant and blasphemous to Christians as it is to Muslims, nevertheless it has persisted in the minds of Muslims throughout the centuries.

When this subject comes up in discussion, the devout Muslim will often quote from Surah 19 of the Qur'an, which says: "And they (the unbelievers) say: The Beneficent hath taken unto Himself a son. Assuredly ye utter a disastrous thing, whereby almost the heavens are torn, and the earth is split asunder and the mountains fall in ruins, that ye ascribe unto the Beneficent a son, when it is not meet for (the Majesty of) the Beneficent that He should choose a son" (Surah 19, *Maryam*, Mary: 88-92). In other sections of the Qur'an, it is stated that Allah "begetteth not nor was begotten" (Surah 112, *At-Tauhid*, The Unity: 3), and that He "hath taken neither wife nor son" (Surah 72, *Al-Jinn*, The Jinn: 3).

It appears that this deep misunderstanding occurred through the confusion of two different terms for the word "son." In Arabic, the word *walad* means "a physical boy born as a result of the marriage of a man and a woman." Of course, if this term is wrongly applied to the conception and birth of Jesus, it gives a totally false impression of physical sonship. It is obvious that the sovereign God would have no physical relationship with a human being.

The Arabic word *ibin*, however, is the word used for "son" throughout the Arabic New Testament in reference to Jesus' relationship with God. *Ibin-Allah* (Son of God) indicates a strong spiritual relationship between Jesus and God — a spiritual sonship in which Jesus was submissive and obedient to God as His "Heavenly Father." (This entire concept is explained in depth by Dr. Ray G. Register, Jr., in his book listed in the bibliography in Appendix IV.)

It is important for Muslims to learn through this careful definition of sonship that Christians agree with the statements in the Qur'an that God has no "partners" (a physical wife or physical son). Rather, Jesus was the Son of God in the sense that the Qur'an refers to Him as the Word of God and the Spirit of God — in the sense of a spiritual relationship.

In actuality, the Qur'an's treatment of the conception and virgin birth of Jesus makes it very clear that the prophet Muhammad acknowledged the supernatural and holy aspects of the coming of Jesus to earth. In reference to the virgin Mary, the Qur'an states, "And she who was chaste, therefore We breathed into her (something) of Our spirit and made her and her son a token for (all) peoples" (Surah 21, *Al-Anbiya*, The Prophets: 91). Further honor and respect is accorded to Mary in another passage: "And then the angels said: O Mary! Lo! Allah hath chosen thee and made thee pure, and hath preferred thee above (all) the women of creation. . . . She said: My Lord! How can I have a child when no mortal hath touched me? He said: So (it will be). Allah createth what He will. If He decreeth a thing, He saith unto it only: Be! and it is" (Surah 3, *Al-i-'Imran*, The Family of Imran: 42,47).

The Qur'an also points toward the sinless nature of Jesus, for an angel comes to tell Mary, "I am only a messenger of thy Lord, that I may bestow on thee a faultless son" (Surah 19, *Maryam*, Mary: 19). At the same time, the Qur'an acknowledges that Jesus was born through the power of the Holy Spirit of God, not through any human agency: "And Mary, daughter of 'Imran, whose body was chaste, therefore We breathed therein something of Our Spirit" (Surah 66, *At-Tahrim*, Banning: 12). Thus, in a spiritual sense, one who is born with God's Spirit should be called God's Son.

Throughout the Qur'an, Jesus is given the title "Son of Mary," indicating His human connection, while in the gospels of the New Testament the term "Son of man" is used for this purpose. The prophet Muhammad plainly indicates that Jesus was much more than an ordinary prophet, giving Him a unique position wherever He is mentioned throughout the

Qur'an. Not only does the Qur'an indicate that His conception and birth were miraculous, but it also states that He lived a sinless life and performed many miracles:

"When Allah saith: O Jesus, son of Mary! Remember My favour unto thee and unto thy mother; how I strengthened thee with the holy Spirit, so that thou spakest unto mankind in the cradle as in maturity; and how I taught thee the Scripture and Wisdom and the Torah and the Gospel; and how thou didst shape of clay as it were the likeness of a bird by My permission, and didst blow upon it and it was a bird by My permission, and thou didst heal him who was born blind and the leper by My permission; and how thou didst raise the dead by My permission; and how I restrained the Children of Israel from (harming) thee when thou camest unto them with clear proofs, and those of them who disbelieved exclaimed" (Surah 5, *Al-Ma'idah*, The Table Spread: 110).

B. The Christian Response

The unique birth of Jesus Christ, prophesied hundreds of years before, is one of the greatest supernatural events recorded in God's Word. The prophet Isaiah foretold this miracle in Isaiah 7:14: "Therefore the Lord Himself will give you a sign: Behold, a virgin will be with child and bear a son, and she will call His name Immanuel." Isaiah also declared, "For a child will be born to us, a son will be given to us; and the government will rest on His shoulders; and His name will be called Wonderful Counselor, Mighty God, Eternal Father, Prince of Peace" (Isaiah 9:6). The Bible makes it very clear that these titles are reserved for the Son of God.

The human vessel chosen for this tremendous happening was a young virgin named Mary. God the Father bore witness to Christ's Sonship when He sent the angel Gabriel to tell Mary this astounding news, saying, "He will be great, and will be called the Son of the Most High; and the Lord God will give Him the throne of His father David" (Luke 1:32). Mary is called "favored" and "blessed" because of her role in bearing the Son of God: "Blessed among women are you, and blessed is the fruit of your womb! . . . And blessed is she who believed that there would be a fulfillment of what had been spoken to her by the Lord" (Luke 1:42,45).

God's Word states that this conception took place through the power of God Himself, not through any human or physical agency. As it was explained to Mary by the angel, "The Holy Spirit will come upon you, and the power of the Most High will overshadow you; and for that reason the holy offspring shall be called the Son of God" (Luke 1:35). Jesus was therefore different from every other man, in that He was God in the flesh. "The Word became flesh, and dwelt among us," the Gospel of John tells us (John 1:14). This is further clarified in Philippians 2:6,7: ". . . Although He [Jesus] existed in the form of God, [He] did not regard equality with God a thing to be grasped, but emptied Himself, taking the form of a bond-servant, and being made in the likeness of men." Therefore, the Son born to Mary was both fully human and fully divine.

Throughout the ministry of Jesus, others testified repeatedly that He was the Son of God. His disciple Peter declared, "Thou art the Christ, the Son of the living God" (Matthew 16:16). Martha, sister of Lazarus and Mary, affirmed, "Yes, Lord; I have believed that You are the Christ, the Son of God, even He who comes into the world" (John 11:27). On two particular occasions (during the baptism of Jesus and the transfiguration), God the Father solemnly announced in a voice from heaven, "This is My beloved Son, in whom I am well-pleased" (Matthew 3:17, 17:5).

Jesus Himself also gave witness to His Sonship in that He called God His Father. Representative of those many passages is His response to some of the religious critics of His day: "Do you say of Him, whom the Father sanctified and sent into the world, 'You are blaspheming,' because I said, 'I am the Son of God'? If I do not do the works of My Father, do not believe Me; but if I do them, though you do not believe Me, believe the works, that you may know and understand that the Father is in Me, and I in the Father" (John 10:36-38).

Jesus demonstrated on earth the eternal attributes and characteristics which God Himself displays. He exercised divine authority, knew the future as well as the inner thoughts of men's hearts, lived a sinless life, remained changeless in His love, justice and righteousness, and performed miracles by the power of His own will. As He revealed the very nature of God through His life, Jesus explained, "I am in the Father, and the Father is in Me. . . . He who has seen Me has seen the Father.

. . . No one comes to the Father, but through Me" (John 14:11,9,6).

It is therefore clear, on the basis of God's Word, that it is only accurate and appropriate to call Jesus the Son of God — not physically begotten, but spiritually related to God the Father as the living Word. This is one of the central truths of the Christian faith, "that you may believe that Jesus is the Christ, the Son of God; and that believing you may have life in His name" (John 20:31).

SUMMARY #4 — *DID JESUS REALLY DIE ON THE CROSS?*

A. The Muslim Perspective

Perhaps the most controversial event in the life of Jesus Christ throughout the Muslim world is the issue of Christ's crucifixion. Because the Qur'an is not entirely clear on this, numerous interpretations have been made of certain passages. The general assumption accepted through the centuries by Muslims is that God loved His prophet so much that just before the crucifixion, He lifted up Jesus into heaven and allowed someone else made to resemble Him to be crucified in His place.

The key passage from the Qur'an upon which this assumption is based states: "And because of their [the Jews'] disbelief and of their speaking against Mary a tremendous calumny; and because of their saying: We slew the Messiah Jesus, son of Mary, Allah's messenger — They slew him not nor crucified, but it appeared so unto them; and lo! those who disagree concerning it are in doubt thereof; they have no knowledge thereof save pursuit of a conjecture; they slew him not for certain. But Allah took him up unto Himself. Allah was ever Mighty, Wise" (Surah 4, *An-Nisa*, Women: 156-158).

One favored interpretation of this passage explains that even though the Jews claimed to have killed Jesus, "it appeared so unto them," and God made them think that they had crucified Jesus. But by mistake they crucified someone else whom God made to resemble Jesus, such as Judas Iscariot or Simon of Cyrene. Another interpretation proposes that this phrase indicates that God caused the entire event of the crucifixion to be an appearance or resemblance of what it really was so that the Jews could not understand it.

However, a number of other passages in the Qur'an make rather direct reference to the death and resurrection of Jesus. (Since some of these quotations have been somewhat obscured in translation from the Arabic Qur'an, I have italicized phrases which have been carefully defined by the respected Arabist, Dr. Ray G. Register, Jr.) In these verses, the prophet Muhammad seems to affirm not only that Christ died, but also that God Himself overshadowed the event and involved Himself in it. "(And remember) when Allah said: O Jesus! Lo! *I will certainly put you to death [mutawaffyk] and raise you up to Myself*" (Surah 3, *Al-i-'Imran*, The Family of Imran: 55). "I (Jesus) spake unto them only that which Thou commandest me (saying): Worship Allah, my Lord and your Lord. I was a witness of them while I dwelt among them, *and when You put me to death [tawaffaytani]* Thou wast the Watcher over them" (Surah 5, *Al-Ma'idah*, The Table Spread: 117).

Perhaps one of the clearest declarations in the Qur'an on this question is in the words attributed to Jesus Himself: "Peace on me the day I was born, and the day I die, and the day I shall be raised alive! Such was Jesus, son of Mary, (this is) a statement of the truth concerning which they doubt" (Surah 19, *Maryam*, Mary: 33,34).

B. The Christian Response

The cross of Jesus Christ is the central point of Christianity. As the only bridge across the chasm between a holy God and sinful man, the cross satisfies the demands of a just God for the punishment of man's sins. At the same time, through the shed blood of the sinless Lamb of God, it demonstrates the compassion of a loving God Who Himself paid the penalty of sin for the whole world.

From the beginning of creation, when Adam and Eve grieved God by their sin of disobedience, God in His love planned the death of His Son to accomplish the redemption of mankind. "For as in Adam all die, so also in Christ all shall be made alive" (I Corinthians 15:22). Moments after the Lord God confronted Adam and Eve with their sin in the Garden of Eden, He announced the first prophecy of the coming of Christ (Genesis 3:15). And that same day, blood was shed for the first time as the sign of atonement when God provided clothing from animal skins for Adam and Eve.

Throughout the Old Testament, God continued to reveal many prophecies and to institute symbolic sacrifices which foretold the sacrificial death of Christ on the cross and His victory over death through the resurrection three days later. These included the bronze serpent raised by Moses in the wilderness, the elaborate and repeated sin offerings and the requirement of a perfect sacrificial lamb without spot or blemish. With remarkable detail, David the psalmist described the painful realities of death by crucifixion in Psalm 22, hundreds of years before this gruesome form of execution came into use. Other details of Christ's trial, death and burial were revealed through the prophet Isaiah (particularly in Chapter 53) and other Old Testament prophets.

In the Levitical law, God had ordained that blood must be shed in order for man's sin to be forgiven. "For the life of the flesh is in the blood, and I have given it to you on the altar to make atonement for your souls; for it is the blood by reason of the life that makes atonement" (Leviticus 17:11). This truth is again repeated in the New Testament: ". . . Without shedding of blood there is no forgiveness" (Hebrews 9:22). One of the most powerful Old Testament symbols of the coming of the sacrificial Lamb of God was the institution of the Passover, when the Angel of Death "passed over" every home protected by the blood of the Passover Lamb on the doorposts (Exodus 12:1-13).

In a totally unique way, Jesus met God's requirements as the perfect Lamb of God sacrificed for the sins of the world. Jesus was holy and sinless from His birth, and throughout His life the Bible tells us that He never sinned. The New Testament says that He "has been tempted in all things as we are, yet without sin" (Hebrews 4:15). Jesus even challenged His enemies to name or prove His sins, but they were silent before Him (John 8:46). In every way, Jesus met the requirements of God's holy justice for a sinless sacrifice, for the holy blood of the Lamb of God.

It was because Jesus was no ordinary man that His death on the cross was unique. The Word of God tells what happened when Christ died on the cross: "The veil of the temple was torn in two from top to bottom, and the earth shook; and the rocks were split, and the tombs were opened" (Matthew 27:51,52), and darkness fell upon all the land for three hours at midday.

All this caused the frightened Roman centurion who was supervising the crucifixion to exclaim, "Truly this was the Son of God!" (Matthew 27:54).

Upon the cross God made Jesus "who knew no sin to be sin on our behalf, that we might become the righteousness of God in Him" (II Corinthians 5:21). The declaration of John the Baptist at Jesus' baptism still resounds today, "Behold, the Lamb of God who takes away the sin of the world!" (John 1:29).

SUMMARY #5 — *HOW CAN A PERSON EXPERIENCE FORGIVENESS OF SINS?*

A. The Muslim Perspective

Throughout all the religions of the world, we find more or less general agreement that man is sinful and must somehow make appeasement for those sins to God (or an array of pagan gods). As one of the strong monotheistic faiths, Islam pictures very graphically the prevailing concept of forgiveness found in all religious systems apart from Christianity. Basically, Islam states that man must somehow satisfy God's judgment for his sins through his own efforts or good works.

The Qur'an teaches clearly, "Every soul will taste of death. And ye will be paid on the Day of Resurrection only that which ye have fairly earned. Whoso is removed from the Fire and is made to enter Paradise, he indeed is triumphant" (Surah 3, *Al-i-'Imran*, The Family of Imran: 185). As the prophet Muhammad explained it, on the Judgment Day God will judge each individual with a set of just balances. Each person's fate will be decided when his good deeds are weighed on the balances against his bad deeds, thus determining whether he is sent to eternal hell or everlasting paradise.

When the issues of sin, forgiveness and atonement are mentioned in the Qur'an, the emphasis is always upon the necessity of doing as many good works as possible during life. This is in order to outweigh the sins which the just, all-knowing God will have accumulated for each person at the Day of Judgment. Because the Qur'an teaches that sin is more powerful than man and that it is impossible for men to conquer sin, it is therefore vital that the devout Muslim do a great number of good works to counterbalance all his sins.

Many categories and degrees of sin are defined in the Qur'an, where at least 15 different Arabic words are used for "sin." One verse, for example, uses three different terms in one sentence: "And whoso committeth a delinquency [*khati'a*] or crime, then throweth (the blame) thereof upon the innocent, hath burdened himself with falsehood [*bahtan*] and a flagrant crime [*ithm*]" (Surah 4, *An-Nisa*, Women: 112).

The eminent Muslim commentator, Al-Imam ar-Razi, has carefully defined the difference between these words for sin. *Al-khati'a*, he explains, is a small, forbidden sin, either premeditated or otherwise, which affects the sinner himself. *Al-bahtan* is the casting of suspicion on an innocent person, a sin that is censured by all and will be punished severely in eternity. *Al-ithm* is a great sin which is deliberate and premeditated and which is a sin against others, such as murder and injustice.

In the Qur'an, atonement and forgiveness have different meanings. Atonement is defined as a "covering" in this world, while forgiveness is the ultimate removal of sins on the Day of Resurrection. The Muslim is concerned mostly with forgiveness, which he can obtain through doing good works. It is recorded in the Hadith (traditional sayings attributed to the prophet Muhammad) that the prophet Muhammad once said to Mua'th Ibn Jabal, "If you do an evil deed, do also beside it a good deed, and it will be blotted out."

Consequently, throughout the Qur'an are found various lists of good works which are sufficient to cancel out one's sins and earn forgiveness. These include giving of alms, fasting, pilgrimage to "the House of Allah" (Mecca), reading and memorizing the Qur'an, "striving in the way of Allah" to protect and promote Islam and saying the creed. When such deeds are performed according to the instructions of the Qur'an, the promise is given, "Allah hath prepared for them forgiveness and a vast reward" (Surah 33, *Al-Ahzab*, The Clans: 35).

When a person needs to obtain forgiveness for the sin of killing (provided that it is accidental), he can either set free a slave and pay blood-money to the murdered person's family or "whoso hath not the wherewithal must fast two consecutive months" (Surah 4, *An-Nisa*, Women: 92). To obtain forgiveness for a false oath, an individual can feed 10 needy people — just as he would feed his own family — or clothe 10 people, or set free a slave, or fast for three days. However, there are three sins which the Qur'an specifies cannot be forgiven under any circumstances: apostasy, killing a believer and polytheism (*shirk*). For these sins no restitution can be accepted.

The prophet Muhammad taught that God is merciful, but only to those who truly submit themselves to all of the laws of Islam as revealed in the Qur'an. "And when the Qur'an is recited, give ear to it and pay heed, that ye may obtain mercy" (Surah 7, *Al-A'raf*, The Heights: 204). Thus, forgiveness in Islam, while it is hopefully anticipated, remains tentative and uncertain until the final weighing of the balances on the Day of Judgment.

B. The Christian Response

The Christian faith presents a striking contrast in regard to the solution to man's sinful condition and the need for God's forgiveness. God's Word teaches that our holy, just and yet loving God has bridged the great gap which separates sinful man from Him by sending His Son Jesus to die on the cross in our place to pay the penalty for our sins. This is the precious truth of John 3:16, "For God so loved the world, that He gave His only begotten Son, that whoever believes in Him should not perish, but have eternal life."

The Bible makes it clear that even though most men believe that they are seeking after God and trying to please Him through their good works, it is not possible for anyone to achieve salvation that way. It is *God* who is seeking for man, even as Jesus declared, "The Son of Man has come to seek and to save that which was lost" (Luke 19:10). Through the shed blood of His perfect Lamb, the Lord Jesus Christ, God offers to sinful man a free pardon.

We learn in the book of Romans, "We aren't saved from sin's grasp by knowing the commandments of God, because we can't and don't keep them, but God put into effect a different plan to save us. He sent His own Son in a human body like ours — except that ours are sinful — and destroyed sin's control over us by giving Himself as a sacrifice for our sins. . . . Those who are still under the control of their old sinful selves, bent on following their old evil desires, can never please God.

But you are not like that. You are controlled by your new nature. . . . Your spirit will live, for Christ has pardoned it" (Romans 8:3,8-10, LB).

In order to experience God's forgiveness, therefore, we must begin by admitting our lost state — our helpless inability to do anything worthwhile in God's sight to attain salvation. The Bible says, "For all have sinned and fall short of the glory of God" (Romans 3:23). The prophet Isaiah wrote, "For all of us have become like one who is unclean, and all our righteous deeds are like a filthy garment" (Isaiah 64:6). No matter how righteous we try to be, we are condemned by James 2:10: "For whoever keeps the whole law and yet stumbles in one point, he has become guilty of all." Moreover, Jesus defined sin as an issue of the heart and attitude, not just the outward action — thus condemning anger along with murder, and lust along with adultery (Matthew 5:21-48).

Once we recognize our sin, we then receive God's free gift of forgiveness and eternal life which was purchased through the death and resurrection of Jesus Christ. By this act of faith, we become children of God, according to His promise: "But as many as received Him, to them He gave the right to become children of God, even to those who believe in His name" (John 1:12). This truth is further clarified in Ephesians 2:8-10: "Because of His kindness you have been saved through trusting Christ. And even trusting is not of yourselves: it too is a gift from God. Salvation is not a reward for the good we have done, so none of us can take any credit for it. It is God Himself who has made us what we are and given us new lives from Christ Jesus" (LB).

The marvel of salvation in Christ is simply that the crucified and risen Lord Jesus Christ comes, through the power of the Holy Spirit, to live His life within every person who accepts Christ's payment on the cross for his sins. Whereas the prophet Muhammad said, "Do good to live," Jesus says, "Live a new life to do good."

The only condition that God demands for salvation is that we accept His Son. "God has given us eternal life, and this life is in His Son. He who has the Son has the life; he who does not have the Son of God does not have the life" (I John 5:11,12). Grace plus nothing else at all is salvation, but grace plus any good works is heresy, for Hebrews 10:12 tells us, "He (Christ)

. . . offered one sacrifice for sins for all time."

Through the exercise of God's supernatural love and power, man can experience total forgiveness by a just God. The Word of God sums up this truth in Romans 5:8-11: "But God demonstrates His own love toward us, in that while we were yet sinners, Christ died for us. Much more then, having now been justified by His blood, we shall be saved from the wrath of God through Him. For if while we were enemies, we were reconciled to God through the death of His Son, much more, having been reconciled, we shall be saved by His life. And not only this, but we also exult in God through our Lord Jesus Christ, through whom we have now received the reconciliation."

In order to make the wonderful discovery of knowing Jesus Christ personally, through which you will find assurance that your sins are forgiven and you are going to heaven, please read "Have You Heard of the Four Spiritual Laws?" in Appendix II.

APPENDIX II

Have You Heard of the
Four Spiritual Laws?

Just as there are physical laws that govern the physical universe, so are there spiritual laws which govern your relationship with God.

LAW ONE

GOD **LOVES** YOU, AND HAS A WONDERFUL **PLAN** FOR YOUR LIFE.

(References contained in this booklet should be read in context from the Bible, God's Word, wherever possible.)

God's Love

God says, "I have loved you with an everlasting love; therefore I have drawn you with lovingkindness" (Jeremiah 31:3).

God's Plan

(Christ speaking) "I came that they might have life, and might have it abundantly" (that it might be full and meaningful) (John 10:10).

Why is it that most people are not experiencing the abundant life? Because . . .

LAW TWO

MAN IS **SINFUL** AND **SEPARATED** FROM GOD. THEREFORE, HE CANNOT KNOW AND EXPERIENCE GOD'S LOVE AND PLAN FOR HIS LIFE.

Man Is Sinful

"For all have sinned and fall short of the glory of God" (Romans 3:23).

Man was created to have fellowship with God; but, because of his stubborn self-will, he chose to go his own independent way, and fellowship with God was broken. This self-will, characterized by an attitude of active rebellion or passive indifference, is an evidence of what the Bible calls sin.

Man Is Separated

"For the wages of sin is death" (spiritual separation from God) (Romans 6:23).

170

God is holy and man is sinful. A great gap separates the two. Man is continually trying to reach God and the abundant life through his own efforts — for example, good works, ethics, philosophy, etc. But despite all his efforts, man is not able to bridge this gap.

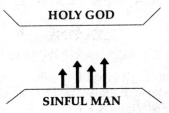

The third law gives us the only answer to this problem . . .

LAW THREE

JESUS CHRIST IS GOD'S **ONLY** PROVISION FOR MAN'S SIN. THROUGH HIM YOU CAN KNOW AND EXPERIENCE GOD'S LOVE AND PLAN FOR YOUR LIFE.

He Is Unique

More than 300 prophecies concerning the details of Jesus Christ's life, all made through prophets who lived hundreds of years before Him, were fulfilled exactly in His life:

1. His unique birth of the virgin Mary (Luke 1:30-35).
2. His sinless life, miracles and incomparable teachings (I Peter 2:22; Matthew 9:35).
3. His sacrifice on the cross for our sins (Romans 5:8).
4. His victorious resurrection from the dead, and His ascension into heaven.

"Christ died for our sins . . . He was buried . . . He was raised on the third day, according to the Scriptures . . . He appeared to Peter, then to the twelve. After that He appeared to more than five hundred . . ." (I Corinthians 15:3-6).

All of these truths point to the fact that . . .

He Is the Only Way to God

"Jesus said to him, 'I am the way, and the truth, and the life; no one comes to the Father, but through Me' " (John 14:6).

John the Baptist testified concerning Jesus, "Behold, the Lamb of God who takes away the sin of the world!" (John 1:29).

God has bridged the gap which separates us from Him by sending Jesus Christ, the Lamb of God, to die on the cross in our place to pay the penalty for our sins.

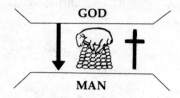

"For God so loved the world, that He gave His only begotten Son, that whoever believes in Him should not perish, but have eternal life" (John 3:16).

"He (Christ) . . . offered one sacrifice for sins for all time" (Hebrews 10:12).

It is not enough just to know these three laws . . .

LAW FOUR

WE MUST INDIVIDUALLY **RECEIVE** JESUS CHRIST AS SAVIOR AND LORD; THEN WE CAN KNOW AND EXPERIENCE GOD'S LOVE AND PLAN FOR OUR LIVES.

We Must Receive Christ

"But as many as received Him, to them He gave the right to become children of God, even to those who believe in His name" (John 1:12).

We Receive Christ Through Faith

"For by grace you have been saved through faith; and that not of yourselves, it is the gift of God; not as a result of works, that no one should boast" (Ephesians 2:8,9).

When We Receive Christ, We Experience a New Birth (Read John 3:1-8).

We Receive Christ by Personal Invitation

(Christ is speaking) "Behold, I stand at the door and knock; if any one hears My voice and opens the door, I will come in to him" (Revelation 3:20). Receiving Christ involves turning to God — repentance — and trusting Christ to come into our lives, to forgive our sins and to make us what He wants us to be. It is not enough to give mental agreement to His claims, nor to have an emotional experience. We receive Jesus Christ by faith, as an act of the will.

These two hearts represent two kinds of lives:

SELF-CONTROLLED LIFE

S—Self on the throne
†—Christ is outside the life
•—Interests controlled by self, often resulting in discord and frustration

CHRIST-CONTROLLED LIFE

†—Christ on the throne of the life
S—Self dethroned
•—Interests under control of Infinite God, resulting in harmony with God's plan.

Which heart best represents your life?

Which heart would you like to have represent your life?

The following explains how you can receive Christ:

YOU CAN RECEIVE CHRIST RIGHT NOW THROUGH A PRAYER OF FAITH

(Prayer is talking with God)

God knows your heart and is not so concerned with your words as He is with the attitude of your heart. The following is a suggested prayer of faith:

"Lord Jesus, I need You. Thank You for dying on the cross for my sins. I confess and repent of my sins, and open the door of my life and receive You as my Savior and Lord. Thank You for forgiving my sins. Take control of the throne of my life. Make me the kind of person You want me to be. Amen."

Does this prayer express the desire of your heart?

If it does, pray this prayer right now by faith, and Christ will come into your life, as He promised.

How to Know that Christ Is in Your Life

As you prayed, did you receive Christ into your life? According to His promise in Revelation 3:20, where is Christ right now in relation to you? Christ said that He would come into your life. Would He mislead you? Therefore, how do you know that God has answered your prayer? (The trustworthiness of God Himself and His Word, the Bible. In other words, God keeps His promises).

The Bible Promises Eternal Life to All Who Receive Christ

"And the witness is this, that God has given us eternal life, and this life is in His Son. He who has the Son has the life; he who does not have the Son of God does not have the life. These things I have written to you who believe in the name of the Son of God, in order that you may know that you have eternal life" (I John 5:11-13).

Thank God often that Christ is in your life and that He will never leave you (Hebrews 13:5). You can know on the basis of His promise that Christ lives in you and that you have eternal life, from the very moment you invite Him in. He will not deceive you.

What about feelings?

DO NOT DEPEND UPON FEELINGS

This promise of God's Word, the Bible — not our feelings — is our authority. The Christian lives by faith (trust) in the trustworthiness of God Himself and His Word. This truck diagram illustrates the relationship between **fact** (God and His Word), **faith** (our trust in God and His Word), and **feeling** (the result of our faith and obedience) (John 14:21).

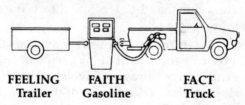

FEELING	FAITH	FACT
Trailer	Gasoline	Truck

The truck will run with or without the trailer. However, it would be useless to attempt to pull the truck by the trailer. In the same way, we, as Christians, do not depend upon feelings or emotions, but we place our faith (trust) in the trustworthiness of God and the promises of His Word.

NOW THAT YOU HAVE RECEIVED CHRIST

The moment that you received Christ by faith, as an act of the will, many things happened, including the following:

1. Christ came into your life (Revelation 3:20 and Colossians 1:27).

2. Your sins were forgiven (Colossians 1:14).

3. You became a child of God (John 1:12).

4. You received eternal life (John 5:24).

5. You began the great adventure for which God created you (John 10:10; II Corinthians 5:17 and I Thessalonians 5:18).

Can you think of anything more wonderful that could happen to you than receiving Christ? Would you like to thank God in prayer right now for what He has done for you? The very act of thanking God demonstrates faith.

Now what?

SUGGESTIONS FOR CHRISTIAN GROWTH

Spiritual growth results from trusting Jesus Christ. "The righteous man shall live by faith" (Galatians 3:11). A life of faith will enable you to trust God increasingly with every detail of your life, and to practice the following:

G Go to God in prayer daily (John 15:7).

R Read God's Word, the Bible, daily (Acts 17:11) — begin with the Gospel of John.

O Obey God moment by moment (John 14:21).

W Witness for Christ by your life and words (Matthew 4:19, John 15:8).

T Trust God for every detail of your life (I Peter 5:7).

H Holy Spirit — allow Him to control and empower your daily life and witness (Galatians 5:16, 17; Acts 1:8).

THE IMPORTANCE OF A GOOD CHURCH

In Hebrews 10:25, we are admonished to forsake not "the assembling of ourselves together . . ." Several logs burn brightly together; but put one aside from the burning flames, and the fire in the log goes out. So it is with your relationship to other Christians. If you do not belong to a local fellowship of believers, do not wait to be invited. Take the initiative; contact or visit a nearby church where Christ is honored and His Word is preached. Start this week, and make plans to attend regularly.

Have You Made the Wonderful Discovery of the Spirit-filled Life?

EVERY DAY CAN BE AN EXCITING ADVENTURE FOR THE CHRISTIAN who knows the reality of being filled with the Holy Spirit and who lives constantly, moment by moment, under His gracious direction.

The Bible tells us that there are three kinds of people:

1. NATURAL MAN
(One who has not received Christ)

"But a natural man does not accept the things of the Spirit of God; for they are foolishness to him, and he cannot understand them, because they are spiritually appraised" (I Corinthians 2:14).

SELF-DIRECTED LIFE
S—Ego or finite self is on the throne
†—Christ is outside the life
•—Interests are directed by self, often resulting in discord and frustration

2. SPIRITUAL MAN
(One who is directed and empowered by the Holy Spirit)

"But he who is spiritual appraises all things . . ." (I Corinthians 2:15).

CHRIST-DIRECTED LIFE
†—Christ is in the life and on the throne
S—Self is yielding to Christ
•—Interests are directed by Christ, resulting in harmony with God's plan

3. CARNAL MAN
(One who has received Christ, but who lives in defeat because he trusts in his own efforts to live the Christian life)

"And I, brethren, could not speak to you as to spiritual

men, but as to carnal men, as to babes in Christ. I gave you milk to drink, not solid food; for you were not yet able to receive it. Indeed, even now you are not yet able, for you are still carnal. For since there is jealousy and strife among you, are you not fleshly, and are you not walking like mere men?" (I Corinthians 3:1-3).

SELF-DIRECTED LIFE
S—Self is on the throne
†—Christ dethroned and not allowed to direct the life
•—Interests are directed by self, often resulting in discord and frustration

1. GOD HAS PROVIDED FOR US AN ABUNDANT AND FRUITFUL CHRISTIAN LIFE.

Jesus said, "I came that they might have life, and might have it abundantly" (John 10:10).

"I am the vine, you are the branches; he who abides in Me, and I in him, he bears much fruit; for apart from Me you can do nothing" (John 15:5).

"But the fruit of the Spirit is love, joy, peace, patience, kindness, goodness, faithfulness, gentleness, self-control; against such things there is no law" (Galatians 5:22,23).

"But you shall receive power when the Holy Spirit has come upon you; and you shall be My witnesses both in Jerusalem, and in all Judea and Samaria, and even to the remotest part of the earth" (Acts 1:8).

THE SPIRITUAL MAN — Some personal traits which result from trusting God:

Christ-centered	Love
Empowered by the Holy Spirit	Joy
Introduces others to Christ	Peace
Effective prayer life	Patience
Understands God's Word	Kindness
Trusts God	Faithfulness
Obeys God	Goodness

The degree to which these traits are manifested in the life depends upon the extent to which the Christian trusts the

Lord with every detail of his life, and upon his maturity in Christ. One who is only beginning to understand the ministry of the Holy Spirit should not be discouraged if he is not as fruitful as more mature Christians who have known and experienced this truth for a longer period.

Why is it that most Christians are not experiencing the abundant life?

2. CARNAL CHRISTIANS CANNOT EXPERIENCE THE ABUNDANT AND FRUITFUL CHRISTIAN LIFE.

The carnal man trusts in his own efforts to live the Christian life:

A. He is either uninformed about, or has forgotten, God's love, forgiveness, and power (Romans 5:8-10; Hebrews 10:1-25; I John 1; 2:1-3; II Peter 1:9; Acts 1:8).

B. He has an up-and-down spiritual experience.

C. He cannot understand himself — he wants to do what is right, but cannot.

D. He fails to draw upon the power of the Holy Spirit to live the Christian life.

(I Corinthians 3:1-3; Romans 7:15-24; 8:7; Galatians 5:16-18)

THE CARNAL MAN — Some or all of the following traits may characterize the Christian who does not fully trust God:

Ignorance of his spiritual heritage
Unbelief
Disobedience
Loss of love for God and for others
Poor prayer life
No desire for Bible study
Legalistic attitude

Impure thoughts
Jealousy
Guilt
Worry
Discouragement
Critical spirit
Frustration
Aimlessness

(The individual who professes to be a Christian but who continues to practice sin should realize that he may not be a Christian at all, according to I John 2:3, 3:6, 9; Ephesians 5:5.)

The third truth gives us the only solution to this problem . . .

3. **JESUS PROMISED THE ABUNDANT AND FRUITFUL LIFE AS THE RESULT OF BEING FILLED (DIRECTED AND EMPOWERED) BY THE HOLY SPIRIT.**

The Spirit-filled life is the Christ-directed life by which Christ lives His life in and through us in the power of the Holy Spirit (John 15).

A. One becomes a Christian through the ministry of the Holy Spirit, according to John 3:1-8. From the moment of spiritual birth, the Christian is indwelt by the Holy Spirit at all times (John 1:12; Colossians 2:9, 10; John 14:16, 17). **Though all Christians are indwelt by the Holy Spirit, not all Christians are filled (directed and empowered) by the Holy Spirit.**

B. The Holy Spirit is the source of the overflowing life (John 7:37-39).

C. The Holy Spirit came to glorify Christ (John 16:1-15). When one is filled with the Holy Spirit, he is a true disciple of Christ.

D. In His last command before His ascension, Christ promised the power of the Holy Spirit to enable us to be witnesses for Him (Acts 1:1-9).

How, then, can one be filled with the Holy Spirit?

4. **WE ARE FILLED (DIRECTED AND EMPOWERED) BY THE HOLY SPIRIT BY FAITH; THEN WE CAN EXPERIENCE THE ABUNDANT AND FRUITFUL LIFE WHICH CHRIST PROMISED TO EACH CHRISTIAN.**

You can appropriate the filling of the Holy Spirit **right now** if you:

A. Sincerely desire to be directed and empowered by the Holy Spirit (Matthew 5:6; John 7:37-39).

B. Confess your sins.

By **faith** thank God that He **has** forgiven all of your sins — past, present, and future — because Christ died for you (Colossians 2:13-15; I John 1; 2:1-3; Hebrews 10:1-17).

C. Present every area of your life to God (Romans 12:1, 2).

D. By **faith** claim the fullness of the Holy Spirit, according to:

1. HIS COMMAND — Be filled with the Spirit.
"And do not get drunk with wine, for that is dissipation, but be filled with the Spirit" (Ephesians 5:18).

2. HIS PROMISE — He will always answer when we pray according to His will. "And this is the confidence which we have before Him, that, if we ask anything according to His will, He hears us. And if we know that He hears us in whatever we ask, we know that we have the requests which we have asked from Him" (I John 5:14, 15).

Faith can be expressed through prayer . . .

HOW TO PRAY IN FAITH TO BE FILLED WITH THE HOLY SPIRIT

We are filled with the Holy Spirit by **faith** alone. However, true prayer is one way of expressing your faith. The following is a suggested prayer:

"Dear Father, I need You. I acknowledge that I have been directing my own life and that, as a result, I have sinned against You. I thank You that You have forgiven my sins through Christ's death on the cross for me. I now invite Christ to again take His place on the throne of my life. Fill me with the Holy Spirit as You **commanded** me to be filled, and as You **promised** in Your Word that You would do if I asked in faith. I pray this in the name of Jesus. As an expression of my faith, I now thank You for directing my life and for filling me with the Holy Spirit."

Does this prayer express the desire of your heart? If so, bow in prayer and trust God to fill you with the Holy Spirit **right now.**

HOW TO KNOW THAT YOU ARE FILLED (DIRECTED AND EMPOWERED) BY THE HOLY SPIRIT

Did you ask God to fill you with the Holy Spirit? Do you know that you are now filled with the Holy Spirit? On what authority? (On the trustworthiness of God Himself and His Word: Hebrews 11:6; Romans 14:22, 23.)

Do not depend upon feelings. The promise of God's Word, not our feelings, is our authority. The Christian lives by faith (trust) in the trustworthiness of God Himself and His Word. This train diagram illustrates the relationship between **fact** (God and His Word), **faith** (our trust in God and His Word), and **feeling** (the result of our faith and obedience) (John 14:21).

The train will run with or without the caboose. However, it would be futile to attempt to pull the train by the caboose. In the same way, we, as Christians, do not depend upon feelings or emotions, but we place our faith (trust) in the trustworthiness of God and the promises of His Word.

HOW TO WALK IN THE SPIRIT

Faith (trust in God and in His promises) is the only means by which a Christian can live the Spirit-directed life. As you continue to trust Christ moment by moment:

A. Your life will demonstrate more and more of the fruit of the Spirit (Galatians 5:22, 23) and will be more and more conformed to the image of Christ (Romans 12:2; II Corinthians 3:18).

B. Your prayer life and study of God's Word will become more meaningful.

C. You will experience His power in witnessing (Acts 1:8).

D. You will be prepared for spiritual conflict against the world (I John 2:15-17); against the flesh (Galatians 5:16, 17); and against Satan (I Peter 5:7-9; Ephesians 6:10-13).

E. You will experience His power to resist temptation and sin (I Corinthians 10:13; Philippians 4:13; Ephesians 1:19-23; 6:10; II Timothy 1:7; Romans 6:1-16).

SPIRITUAL BREATHING

By faith you can continue to experience God's love and forgiveness.

If you become aware of an area of your life (an attitude or an action) that is displeasing to the Lord, even though you are walking with Him and sincerely desiring to serve Him, simply thank God that He has forgiven your sins — past, present and future — on the basis of Christ's death on the cross. Claim His love and forgiveness by faith and continue to have fellowship with Him.

If you retake the throne of your life through sin — a definite act of disobedience — breathe spiritually.

Spiritual breathing (exhaling the impure and inhaling the pure) is an exercise in faith and enables you to continue to experience God's love and forgiveness.

1. **Exhale** — confess your sin — agree with God concerning your sin and thank Him for His forgiveness of it, according to I John 1:9 and Hebrews 10:1-25. Confession involves repentance — a change in attitude and action.

2. **Inhale** — surrender the control of your life to Christ, and appropriate (receive) the fullness of the Holy Spirit by faith. Trust that He now directs and empowers you, according to the **command** of Ephesians 5:18 and the **promise** of I John 5:14, 15.

A SUGGESTED BIBLIOGRAPHY

The following resource materials in English are recommended for a basic background in understanding Islam and sharing the love of Jesus Christ with peoples of the Middle East.

INTRODUCTION TO ISLAM

A Brief History of Islam – A Christian Interpretation by Harry Boer. Ibadan, Nigeria: Daystar Press, 1969.

Introducing Islam by J. Christy Wilson. New York: Friendship Press, 1959.

Islam in Modern History by Wilfred Cantwell Smith. Princeton University Press, 1957.

Mohammedanism – An Historical Study by H. A. R. Gibb. Oxford University Press, 1973.

Shorter Encyclopedia of Islam by H. A. R. Gibb and J. H. Kramers, Eds. Cornell University Press, 1953.

The Legacy of Islam by J. Schacht and Bosworth, Eds. Oxford University Press, 1974.

What is Islam? by W. Montgomery Watt. London: Longmans, Green & Co., Ltd., 1968.

THE QUR'AN

Companion to the Qur'an by W. Montgomery Watt. London: George Allen and Unwin Ltd., 1967.

Introduction to the Qur'an by Richard Bell. Edinburgh University Press, 1953.

The Events of the Qur'an by Kenneth Cragg. London: George Allen and Unwin Ltd., 1971.

The Koran Interpreted by Arthur J. Arberry. New York: Macmillan, 1964.

The Meaning of the Glorious Koran by Mohammed Marmaduke Pickthall. New York: Dover Publications, 1977.

The Qur'an as Scripture by Arthur Jeffrey. New York: Russell Moore Co., 1952.

CHRISTIANITY AND ISLAM

A Christian's Response to Islam by William M. Miller. Nutley, New Jersey: Presbyterian and Reformed Publishing Co., 1976.

"Christianity and Islam" series by David Brown & Gordon Huelin. London: S.P.C.K.

Christianity Explained to Muslims, A Manual for Christian Workers by L. Bevan Jones. Calcutta: YMCA Publishing House, 1952.

Dialogue and Interfaith Witness with Muslims by Ray G. Register, Jr. Kingsport, Tennessee: Moody Books Inc., 1979.

Explaining the Gospel to Muslims by John Crossley. London: Lutterworth Press, 1960.

Jesus in the Qur'an by Geoffrey Parrinder. London: Faber and Faber, 1965.

Reaching Muslims Today, A Short Handbook. North Africa Mission, 1976.

Share Your Faith with a Muslim by Charles R. Marsh. Chicago: Moody Press, 1975.

The Balance of Truth (Mizanu'l Haqq) by C. G. Pfander. Beirut, 1974.

The Call of the Minaret by Kenneth Cragg. London: Oxford University Press, 1964.

The Christian Approach to the Moslem, A Historical Study by James T. Addison. New York: Columbia University Press, 1942.

The Fortress and the Fire, Jesus Christ and the Challenge of Islam by Phil Parshall. Bombay: Gospel Literature Service, 1975.

The Gospel and Islam: A 1978 Compendium by Don M. McCurry, ed. Monrovia, California: MARC, 1979.

The Practical Approach to Muslims by Jens Christensen. North Africa Mission, 1977.

CHRISTIAN LITERATURE WRITTEN FOR MUSLIMS

Beliefs and Practices of Christians (A Letter to a Friend) by William M. Miller. Lahore: Masihi Isha'at Khana, 1972.

Can We Know? by Dale and Elaine Rhoton. Fort Washington, Pa.: Christian Literature Crusade, 1972.

"Have You Heard of the Four Spiritual Laws?" by Dr. Bill Bright. Adapted for the Middle East, 1977.

The God Who Speaks to Man. Oak Park, Ill.: Emmaus Bible School, 1973.

The Life and Teaching of Jesus the Messiah by Dennis E. Clark. Elgin: Dove Publications, 1977.

The True Path, Seven Muslims Make Their Greatest Discovery by Mark Hanna. Colorado Springs: International Doorways Publications, 1975.